fifties coffee shop

Googie

architecture

alan hess

CHRONICLE BOOKS

Photo credits

Anshen and Allen 53
Anshen and Allen; Ernest Braun, photographer 52
Armét, Davis and Newlove 11,36,72,76,83,85
Armét, Davis and Newlove; Jack Laxer 30,38,47,71
    72,74,75,79,81,82,84,85,86,93,95
Armét, Davis and Newlove; Merge Studios 38,73,78
Armét, Davis and Newlove; Sinitzin, photographer 128
Armét, Davis and Newlove; R. Wenkam, photographer 93
California Neon 47,131
Chrysler Historical Collection 54,55,57,58,132
P. B. DeRosa 41
Mike Fink 7,13,43,69,74,80,87,88,96,101,111
Charles Fish 100,104
Ford Industrial Archives 54
Buckminster Fuller Institute, Los Angeles 19,20
Garber Sturges, photographers 65
General Motors Corporation 57,59
Bruce Goff Archives 83
Alan Hess 5,9,10,12,14,16,17,18,25,26,32,35,36,37,
    40,43,44,45,46,56,58,70,76,80,82,85,89,90,91,
    92,96,97,99,102,103,106,107,111,114,115,118,120,
    122,124,126,127,128,129,130,132
KTLA Los Angeles, copyright 1952 33
John Lautner 66
The MIT Museum 50,51
Ray Quiel 98
Ralph Rapson 48
Reibsamen Nickels and Rex; Marks Photographers 70
Reibsamen Nickels and Rex; Merge Studios 67
Reibsamen Nickels and Rex; George Szanik,
    photographer 67,68
Reibsamen Nickels and Rex; Teske, photographer 64
Security Pacific National Bank Photograph Collection,
    Los Angeles Public Library 29
Emmett Shipman 87
Julius Shulman 6,60,70
Tim Street-Porter 41,71,81,91,112,117,123,125,131
Tombrock Corporation 27
Western History Collection, Natural History Museum
    of Los Angeles County, Seaver Center for
    Western History Research 21
Eric Wright 8,22,23

to Barbara and Charles Hess

Printed and bound in Japan by Toppan
Printing Co., Ltd., Tokyo

Library of Congress Cataloging-in-Publication Data
Hess, Alan.
    Googie: fifties coffee shop architecture.
    Bibliography: p.
    Includes index.
    1. Coffee-houses – United States. 2. Car washes –
United States. 3. Architecture, Modern – 20th century –
United States. I. Title.
NA7856.H47 1985   725′.71′0973   85-17089
ISBN 0-87701-334-9 (pbk.)
10 9 8 7 6 5 4 3 2 1

Distributed in Canada by
Raincoast Books
112 East 3rd Avenue
Vancouver, B.C.
V5T 1C8

Art Direction: Jim Heimann
Cover and Book Design: Mike Fink
Cover Tinting: Dale Sizer
Composition: On Line Typography

Chronicle Books
One Hallidie Plaza
San Francisco, CA 94102

contents

*Bob's Big Boy, 1949, Wayne McAllister,
Riverside Drive at Alameda, Toluca Lake.*

Coffee Dan's, *1954, Douglas Honnold, Wilshire Boulevard at Second, Santa Monica, remodeled.*

foreword

Oh, those names! They fly and swoop, dance and jump, rock and roll—Ship's and Chip's, Googie's and Biff's, Bob's Big Boy, and Tiny Naylor's, Smorgyburger, Jump N' Jack and the Celestial Motel. We all grew up with them on roadside strips—east, west, north, south.

Except for a few slick high-rise corporate headquarters dear to architects and critics, these roadside and main street eateries, with their tapered columns, cantilevers, vaults, parabolas and boomerangs, represented all most of us knew as modern architecture in the forties and fifties. After we got "good taste" in Fine Arts I and II, we hardly dared look back at the tawdry Modernism of our own callow years.

Historically, one generation has tended to look back with nostalgia and renewed interest to the architecture and popular culture of its grandparents' generation. But since World War II our appetite for the styles of the past has quickened, and in only twenty years we have consumed the Shingle Style and Victoriana, Art Nouveau, Art Deco, Moderne, early Modern, and Beaux Arts, and now we find ourselves looking seriously at the late Modern commercial architecture of the forties and fifties, a mere media blink behind us.

It takes brave historian/critics such as J. B. Jackson, Vincent Scully, and David Gebhard, and architects such as Robert Venturi and Denise Scott Brown and now Alan Hess to venture into this difficult area, where contemporary observation and theorizing, recent history, and an appreciation of the buildings of the everyday landscape come together. When considering architecture so close to our present, the editing effect of time has only begun to work and we are dependent on the subjectivity of our own eyes; neat stylistic categories won't help us much, absolute aesthetic judgments of good and bad, high and low, are less important than a sure sense of time, place, and meaning.

In the fifties the everyday, commercial architectural environment was still relatively ad hoc and unplanned. By the sixties we had urban renewal with a vengeance. On the far side of urban renewal's wholesale destruction of much of the fabric of the American city, we look back on the fifties with a renewed appreciation for the unplanned, the ad hoc, and the humorous.

There is a place for humor in the architectural environment; sometimes fleeting—a billboard weirdly juxtaposed with its surroundings—and sometimes a little more permanent—a hot dog stand in the shape of a hot dog. The application of universal standards or canons of good taste which directed urban renewal can, if we're not careful, remove our opportunity to appreciate the unexpected humor implicit in our pluralistic society, i.e., the other guy's taste culture is always beyond the pale and/or humorous.

Architects and critics who hope to be sensitive observers of our time and place must straddle these contradictory taste cultures. They must learn from Googie's rather than Graves in order to design buildings that neither degrade their users nor seem degraded by people's activities or preferences, and to set architectural diversity within a larger cultural context where extraordinary buildings know their place, and ordinary buildings can be seen to be extraordinary.

Steven Izenour

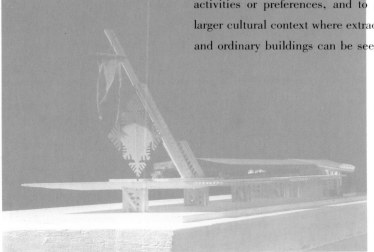

Open Air Market, *1931, Lloyd Wright, Monrovia, project. A fifty-six-foot-high steel truss held the revolving snowflakelike sign of this roadside market. Its bold scale and exposed structure was prophetic of the roadside solutions that the commercial vernacular was to develop in the next three decades.*

preface

Bob's Big Boy, c. 1950, 3130 East Colorado Boulevard, Pasadena, demolished 1982.

The history of the California coffee shop turns out to be my own. My family was one of those that had moved into the new tracts of the San Gabriel Valley during the postwar boom, the ready-made clientele for the newly evolved coffee shop restaurant. Some of my earliest memories are of the leatherette booths of Bob's Big Boy on East Colorado in Pasadena and the cool recesses of Van de Kamp's, drinking a frosted mug of root beer with my grandparents. I remember the glint of light on chrome and windshield through expanses of glass window. Everything shimmered in the brilliant light that poured over the banana trees and palms and Mercurys and stucco walls of Southern California.

The style followed me a few years later to Detroit, where the California coffee shop's modern roofs and acres of glass looked out, incongruously, on snow-covered parking lots alien to the desert setting where they had originated. They testified to the spread of California culture.

Nearby in Detroit was Northland, one of Victor Gruen's first regional shopping malls, which the car culture had spawned, as it had the coffee shop and drive-in. In high school in Chicago's northwest suburbs, I lived near the first outpost of McDonald's outside its western birthplace.

The modern shapes and car-oriented life style of these buildings strongly suggested that the future was getting closer every day. The House of the Future at Disneyland was a wonder, bright with curving walls and thousands of neat gadgets popping out of the wall and up from the floor. I was ready to move in. There was even a rocket ship

Hood ornament, 1955 Cadillac. *The fifties update the centaur: half woman, half rocket.*

in Tomorrowland, a thin, tapering cigar-shaped tube with elegant fins on the end, just like the one in my *Golden Book of Astronomy.* I drew its sleek shape constantly. I also drew sputniks, a favorite kindergarten icon after the first one went up in 1957. It was easy to draw—a circle with hairy spikes coming out of it. The rockets on the first manned space flights didn't really look like the one at Disneyland, but it didn't matter. The sleek Disneyland rocket, poised on the planes of the moon, was a vivid image of the future present that gave a five year old a sense of the excitement of the world around him. Tomorrowland was not just in Anaheim.

Twenty years later, I stumbled back into the California coffee shops while in architecture school at UCLA.

Touring Los Angeles in search of its amazing architecture, I would take a picture of a giant arrow roof, or an old McDonald's or the tremendous butterfly roof of a bowling alley, or the slanty glass walls of a coffee shop. The shapes and forms of Googie still worked: they still had the power to grab the eye. Only gradually as I began tracking down their dates and architects did I realize that the random photos of crazy shapes I had taken were in fact examples of a cohesive style that had dominated Los Angeles in the fifties and sixties. Unconsciously I had been cataloging the style.

With the passage of time, the Googie style became as much a symbol of the fifties as Elvis Presley or a '57 Chevy. Cultural expression is an important role of architecture. But the coffee shops also worked well by other measures of architecture: they solved the functional problems of a car-oriented building imaginatively; they used scale and form to create an urban strip architecture; their complex interior geometries showed an understanding of modern spatial concepts. Though they were not the kind of building given attention in the architectural journals, they helped to mold the appearance of cities nationwide. They were modern architecture, but they were also widely popular, a rare combination in the history of Modernism. They did not simply mimic high art design. The commercial strip itself had generated a fresh, appropriate architecture. It was a commercial vernacular style, because it was a common design language of the public streets, understood by a large cross section of the population.

I had to find out why they looked the way they did. Calling up Bob's Big Boy headquarters, I asked for the name of the architect of their Toluca Lake restaurant, which raised the billboard into art. They told me it was probably Armét, Davis and Newlove, but when I called Eldon Davis, he said no, they hadn't. "But we did design Johnie's and Norm's and Conrad's and Denny's and Huddle's and Carolina Pines," and he proceeded to list most of the coffee shops I had admired. Suddenly all the pieces fell into place. I had struck the mother lode of fifties architecture.

Elias Brothers Big Boy, 1961, Armét and Davis, Dearborn, Michigan.

*McDonald's, 1953, Stanley C. Meston, 10207
Lakewood Boulevard at Florence, Downey.*

Of the many people who have helped in the course of my research and writing, I am indebted to Eldon Davis, P. K. Reibsamen, Stanley Meston, and Charles Fish for generously providing crucial information and photos that made this book possible. Many additional architects, designers, restaurant owners, and others directly involved in roadside commercial architecture in the fifties helped tremendously too, including John Lautner, Richard McDonald, Esther McCoy, Julius Shulman, Roger Williams, Bud Landon, Stan Abrams, Robert Wian, Wayne McAllister, Elaine Sewell Jones, Strother MacMinn, James Powers, George Dexter, Paul Davis, Pat DeRosa, Emmett Shipman, Edgardo Contini, Martin Stern, Jr., Merrill Winans, Emiel Becsky, Jack Didion, Alonzo Keathley, Bruce Berghoff, Russell Forester, and Whitney Smith.

Many others provided invaluable archival information, including Darleen Flaherty of the Ford Industrial Archives; Dr. Elizabeth Patrick and Susan Dolin of the University of Nevada; Biljana Delevich and Charles Jordan of General Motors; David Crippen, Cynthia Read-Miller, and Steven Hamp of the Henry Ford Museum; Anna Ganahl and

Don Kubly of Art Center; Steve Leroy of McDonald's Corporation; Spencer Weart of the American Institute of Physics; the Monsanto Corporation; the Massachusetts Institute of Technology; Golden West Broadcasters; the California Historical Society; the Alfred P. Sloan Museum; Tombrock Corporation; Eric Wright; Peter Sauers; Mrs. Glenn Amundsen; Dick Whittington; David DeLong of the Goff Archives; Bruce Torrence, Vince Van de Venter, Norm Fogel, Ray Quiel, Tom Owen, and Bettye Ellison of the Los Angeles Public Library; Barbara Moore and Bill Unger of Jack-In-The-Box; and the Special Collections at the UCLA University Research Library.

I am also grateful for the generous support of Virginia and Wesley Scott, and Shirley and Robert Jeffery who made possible long research visits to far away cities and therefore made this book possible. For their ideas, leads, and encouragement, I thank Dale Furman, Heather Kurze, John Chase, Sara Terry, Stewart McBride, Jim Heimann, Dulce and Steve Carothers, Elizabeth A. T. Smith, Joseph Corn, Brian Horrigan, David and Liz Scott, Joyce Lawrence and the Downey Historical Society, Charles Hosmer, Chester Liebs, Arthur Krim, John Margolies, Michael Corbett, Tim Street-Porter, Ruthann Lehrer and the Los Angeles Conservancy, Roger Honey, Murray Silverstein, Elyse Grinstein, Chris Evans, Jonathan Hess, and especially Barbara Goldstein, editor of *Arts and Architecture*, for recognizing the value of this material and publishing my initial research in a way that did justice to it. Thanks are insufficient to acknowledge the patient and professional typing of Barbara Hess over numerous drafts.

Also important to this book are the writers and critics who first opened the subject of roadside architecture to serious consideration and whose books and lectures have influenced me: Robert Venturi and Denise Scott Brown, David Gebhard, and especially J. B. Jackson.

Perhaps the person most influential on the direction of this book is noted architect and historian John Beach, who ten years ago showed a class of first-year architecture students at UCLA the buildings we didn't even know we had been looking for. The number of ideas I have since borrowed from him consciously or unconsciously is impossible to calculate. As I suspect that I have not put them down with his same astonishing acuity, I must take responsibility for them here.

We are asked to take seriously the architectural taste of real estate speculators, renting agents, and mortgage brokers!

—Alfred Barr, Jr., 1932

introduction

The future ended September 20, 1984. They closed down Ship's coffee shop at midnight, and the bulldozers came in the morning.

For twenty-six years you could see the future at the corner of Glendon and Wilshire in Westwood Village. Ship's had not been subject to the ordinary forces of gravity. It did not need mundane columns and walls to hold up its roof. Some unseen force field had held its hovering roof canopy overhead. Its walls had dematerialized into invisible screens of glass to keep out the weather. The interior was not so much a room as a garden, surrounded by lush subtropical planting. Glowing teardrops and globes, hanging from the pitched ceilings, cast light on rough hewn, cavelike walls. Here Fred Flintstone and George Jetson could meet over a cup of coffee. This future represented the climax of man's dominion over the forces of gravity, heat, cold, sun, and darkness. With his science he was able to temper their vagaries while enjoying their benefits. He had abolished walls as heavy opaque barriers. He had also thrown off the limitations of his own traditional architecture and building practices.

Ship's had been finely tuned to the car culture of Southern California, too. A pavilion in a parking lot, its bold shapes and colorful spaces beckoned to drivers far down the street by offering a protected oasis in the midst of the noise and hustle of traffic. It provided a convenient and fitting stage for a rest and a meal along the arteries of the car city.

Ship's Westwood, 1958, Martin Stern, Jr., 10877 Wilshire Boulevard at Glendon, Los Angeles, demolished 1984.

It had been a people's palace, one of hundreds of coffee shops and drive-ins built nationwide during the fifties and sixties. It had established the technological image of Modernism in the lives of the mass public. It completed the revolution of Walter Gropius, Frank Lloyd Wright, Mies van der Rohe, and Le Corbusier, the Futurists and the Constructivists, the Expressionists and the Bauhaus. And its accomplishments had been dismissed as "Googie."

So the future finally ended that night, a long process over more than a decade. They had started to build the past again. For twenty-six years Ship's and other coffee shops in the California Coffee Shop style had told us about ourselves by showing us in full scale and three dimensions what we once thought our future would look like. By the time it was torn down, we had changed our mind about what our future would be. While it remained we could be reminded of what we had once believed, and reflect on why our future had changed so much.

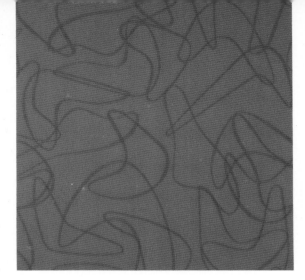

Formica pattern.

Ship's Westwood, *1958, Martin Stern, Jr.,*
10877 Wilshire Boulevard at Glendon, Los
Angeles, demolished 1984.

Pan Pacific Auditorium, *1935, Wurdeman and Becket, 7600 Beverly Boulevard, Los Angeles. William Wurdeman and Welton Becket designed Pan Pacific while working for Plummer and Feil, who designed the first Van de Kamp's drive-in in 1938.*

Nothing in the East compares with the best things of this sort in Los Angeles.

—Henry-Russell Hitchcock, 1940

the '30s

The Streamline Moderne style of the 1930s in Los Angeles was a convincing dress rehearsal for the democratic technological future of the 1950s. Even the Great Depression could not completely dampen the show.

Throughout the depression, the hope of a brighter tomorrow was a popular theme. Advancing technology seemed to offer the most promising road. The evidence of mass production, household appliances, and air travel supported the promise; as a symbol of this new technology, the Streamline Moderne became widely popular.

The smooth Streamline forms carried the eye easily around corners, reducing resistance for efficient movement, a visual metaphor of the reduced wind resistance of streamlined locomotives and airplanes. The teardrop form, its continuous planes submerging individual elements under a single organic shape, became a symbol of the movement, despite the fact it was not, scientifically speaking, the ideal wind-resistant form. It certainly looked like it was; for symbolic purposes of design announcing a new age, that was enough.

Designers were not looking for the scientific fact; they were imagining what invisible forces of speed and energy would look like. In the public mind, streaming lines came to be associated with modern technology. High art critics labeled the Streamline merely cosmetic, but in the public eye its curves relieved some of the austere lines of boxlike Bauhaus modernism.

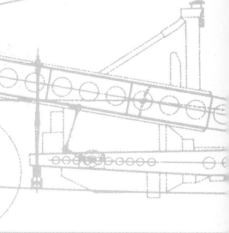

Dymaxion Car #1, *1933, Buckminster Fuller.*
One of several prototype cars that promoted the
streamlined teardrop form in the 1930s.

Chicago's 1933 Century of Progress and New York's 1939 World of Tomorrow expositions helped focus public interest in this future and the Streamline Moderne as its representative. In New York, Norman Bel Geddes's Futurama for General Motors, Henry Dreyfuss's exhibit of Democracity inside the Perisphere and Raymond Loewy's exhibit of a rocket port and his real-life Streamline locomotives, and in Chicago Buckminster Fuller's Dymaxion car and George Fred Keck's House of Tomorrow were seductive images that this hopeful future could be built. But the images of the Streamline were not just in once-in-a-lifetime fairs; they were spread along the streets of cities. Especially in Los Angeles, the architecture, noted Aldous Huxley in 1939, looked "like the pavilions at some endless international exhibition."

Herbert's, Carpenter's, Simon's, Harrold's, Robert's, Van de Kamp's, and other Los Angeles drive-ins set a pattern of bold, futurist, car-oriented architecture that culminated in the coffee shops of the forties and fifties. Early drive-ins in Texas and California had been little more than roadside sheds, but their owners experimented with ways to accommodate and serve many cars, and to attract potential customers. Supported by a growing population and a lot of space to grow in, commercial strategies evolved in dozens of drive-ins and chains in several rapid generations of ad hoc, pragmatic innovations. Catering to the Southern California public's fondness for the mobile life style, drive-ins made it easier for people to patronize roadside restaurants, which in turn encouraged the public's reliance on automobile transportation.

Los Angeles consciously embarked upon a policy of sprawl, even if its extent and consequences were not imagined. The dispersed city was a solution to the congestion of eastern cities.

The climate in Southern California also shaped the drive-in culture. Citizens spent less time preparing for and fighting the elements in order to live. Buildings could be built more quickly and of lighter materials, like wood and stucco, instead of the serious brick or stone used in harsher climates.

Angelenos browsed at outdoor libraries in Pershing Square, enjoyed symphonies under the stars at the Hollywood Bowl, and shopped at open-air markets "where displays of bright fruits, vegetables, and flowers remind easterners of the lavish exhibits at a state fair," noted

a Works Progress Administration survey in 1939. The convertible and the drive-in applied the same principle to the car culture, and architects responded wholeheartedly.

With a firm foundation in his father's architectural ideas, Frank Lloyd Wright's son, Lloyd Wright, set up practice in Los Angeles in the 1920s. He was clearly in tune with the possibilities of the developing car-oriented city; as early as 1928, his Yucca-Vine drive-in stores foreshadowed the drive-ins of the thirties. The upswept corrugated roof of a Yucca-Vine store was distinctive by day and by night, when its reflected light made it visible down the street. A sculptural pylon rose from the polygonal pavilion, its jaunty chevrons precursors of future Simon's, Herbert's, and Carpenter's. A wing stretched out from the main pavilion, with folding doors that completely opened the face of the

Yucca-Vine Market, 1928, Hollywood. Wright used startling industrial materials like corrugated metal and exposed steel columns as the design elements of his building. Metal screened doors pulled across the market front at night, and drapes pulled across it at day to cut the sun.

Yucca-Vine Market, 1928, Lloyd Wright, Yucca near Vine, Hollywood, demolished. Lloyd Wright's design for a drive-in market developed most of the themes of the thirties drive-ins: the central pavilion with its sculptural pylon; integral lighting so the building would stand out by night; the up-to-the-minute modern imagery; the easy access from car to store. The concrete wall to the left still stands, though the site is now a parking lot.

market during the day. The interior's exposed structure and corrugated metal finish were prototypically modern.

A restaurant was distinguished by its clientele and its imagery. The polished Hollywood Regency style of many of the clubs offered the image of sophistication; the twenty-four-hour drive-ins cut democratically across class lines by offering the common denominator of citizenship in the age of speed.

Restaurants offered a wide range of atmospheres, from the society nightclubs like Ciro's and the Trocadero on the Sunset Strip and the fancy dinner houses of La Cienega's restaurant row, to the strip-scaled Tail o' the Pup, the Giant Tamale, and Whizzin's Chili Bowls, with innumerable barbecue pits, greasy spoons, tearooms, cafeterias, and diners in between.

Cafeterias have been traced to Chicago in 1907, but they became popular in Los Angeles when the Boos brothers opened one in 1912.

Clifton's several cafeterias were social institutions, combining gospel charity (you paid what you could afford) with Hollywood fantasy. The building at Olive and Sixth downtown was a cliff with a running waterfall cascading down its facade; inside neon palm trees sprouted next to Polynesian huts.

Also downtown, the Simon brothers ran a chain of dairy lunch counters, modified cafeterias with short-order kitchens, that were popular for lunch with office workers. These operations were the equivalent of today's fast-food restaurants. The Simons decided to follow the trend to move out of downtown to the new car-oriented developments along Wilshire, Sunset, and Ventura boulevards. Carpenter's already had a few drive-ins: one at Sunset and Vine was a polygonal stepped pyramid with the menu lining the steps.

This was before the freeways, and people traveled on surface streets; corners like Sepulveda and Ventura, Fairfax and Wilshire, Pico and Sepulveda carried crosstown traffic and were ideal for drive-ins. Many drive-ins were built on a potentially valuable site to generate money for property taxes until the land appreciated in value and could be sold at a profit. Bill Simon chose Wayne McAllister to design his new drive-in.

Wayne McAllister moved to Los Angeles in the early thirties from his native San Diego and was quickly involved in a succession of restaurant designs, including the Biltmore Bowl nightclub and Lyman's restaurant. Though he had no formal training, McAllister had apprenticed with architects and was already an experienced designer; he had worked on the 1928 Agua Caliente resort over the border in Mexico, a hotel, cafe, and casino with a spa, swimming pool, and racetrack. It was in the Spanish style, but from magazines he was aware of the new Art Deco style developing in Europe, and parts of Agua Caliente reflected the 1925 Exposition des Arts Decoratifs in Paris, which promoted the Art Deco style and produced the Zigzag Moderne.

McAllister designed the first Simon's drive-in in 1935, far from downtown on the northwest corner of Fairfax and Wilshire. The Wilshire District was developing rapidly beside the nearby oil wells and tarpits. A few blocks east at La Brea, the Desmond tower (Gilbert Underwood, 1928), in the stepped-back skyscraper style, and the Wilson building (Meyer and Holler, 1929) formed a core surrounded by parking lots and low-rise markets, car dealerships, theaters, and apartments in Zigzag and Spanish Colonial styles. There were several billboards, angled to the flow of traffic, on vacant lots.

Up Fairfax at the Beverly intersection, the Farmer's Market, in a homey farmhouse style complete with windmill, was just being founded as the ultramodern Simon's pavilion was dropped into place. East on Beverly the Pan Pacific Auditorium (Wurdeman and Becket), in the same Streamline style, was also being completed.

Simon's was followed by Coulter's department store (Stiles O. Clements, 1938), a larger version of the Streamline, nearby. Nineteen forty brought an even more dominating neighbor, May Company department store (A. C. Martin), its corner an elegant five-story gold mosaic cylinder.

Simon's circular plan organized cars like spokes of a wheel, making all customers equally accessible to the carhops and the central kitchen. Its octagonal canopy covered the walkway around the building; in later Simon's, McAllister would extend the canopy even farther to cover more of the cars themselves. A central pylon made the building visible to passing motorists; at night, tubing hidden behind metal louvers created a neon exclamation point.

Dolores Drive-in, *c. 1938, Wilshire Boulevard at La Cienega, Los Angeles, demolished. Dolores', which originally had a central pylon like Simon's and Herbert's, shows the influence McAllister's designs had on other drive-ins.*

"Those were the days of struggling for something exciting and neon was rather new. We had neon everywhere," remembers Stanley Meston, who worked with McAllister on the drive-ins. Neon was used not just for lettering, or pictorially, but as an integrated architectural element to delineate form.

A counter with twelve stools stood inside, with the carhop counter between. The drive-in never closed. Indeed, it couldn't close; there were no doors. Glass windbreaks provided some enclosure. Without equipment, the building cost sixty-five hundred dollars.

Barbecued sandwiches, the meat slow cooked over hickory logs in a central pit, were the main dish. Fried chicken was also popular; the hamburger was not yet respectable.

"Hamburger joints were a dingy type of place," recalls Bob Wian, who opened his first diner across town on Colorado Boulevard in Glendale in 1936, to upgrade the image of the hamburger. His sesame-seed buns, double-decker cheeseburger, and garnish were culinary equivalents of the pylons and neon of drive-ins—they made his diner stand out.

McAllister followed by designing several more Simon's as well as Robert's, Herbert's, McDonnell's, Van de Kamp's, and later Bob's Big Boy. "I tried to do them all," says McAllister. Those he did not design he influenced, like Dolores at La Cienega and Wilshire.

Stanley Meston recalls that McAllister "was one of the most capable men. He was no draftsman, but he had the ability to perceive and then to surround himself with the right people. He knew materials, he knew equipment, he knew how to discuss things with the owner and how to get the end result."

A roadside commercial vernacular style developed. By speaking a popular visual language that a majority of people using the highways could understand, roadside design learned to sell and serve more effectively.

The rise of drive-in restaurants was paralleled by the rise of the auto court and motel, shopping centers, the supermarket, and the drive-in theater. All responded to the same technological and commercial phenomenon, the widespread availability and ownership of the auto. Commerce proved to be highly sensitive to changes in life styles, like the growing car culture, which could be exploited in style or service.

The East Coast Howard Johnson's, started as an ice cream store in the 1920s, pioneered roadside architecture. Though their imagery was comfortably colonial, their bright orange roofs recognized the need for visibility and its effect on design.

The drive-ins of the thirties developed design strategies that the fifties coffee shop was to continue. They recognized that, for a commercial building, advertising is a legitimate function to be expressed in architectural form. To make a relatively small building visible to customers from far down the street, the entire building was conceived as a sign to attract customers. Stands in the shape of fanciful giant objects, animals, fruits, and foods, an architectural onomatopoeia,

Tail o' the Pup, 1938, Milton J. Black, La Cienega Boulevard at Beverly, Los Angeles. Architectural onomatopoeia like this giant hot dog that sells hot dogs was an early commercial vernacular answer to the problem of how to attract car customers. As an eye-catching strategy, the Streamline Moderne replaced mythically scaled food with futuristic modernism.

used bold scale as a design concept in the twenties. McAllister's Simon's introduced more abstract Streamline Moderne forms. The public's eye was becoming more sophisticated.

The Streamline Moderne had been coming into vogue in roadside buildings nationwide. Its modern image, its affinity for the speed and sleekness of the car made it an appropriate style for a totally new building type created by the car culture.

McAllister's Simon's in Los Angeles, however, was a more thoroughly car-oriented design than, for example, the White Towers of the East and Midwest. They shared the curves, shapes, towers, and metal and neon finishes of Streamline, but the White Tower drive-ins had front doors for pedestrians walking in off the sidewalk. Simon's did not even have a door, its open circular plan permitting access from all directions and allowing cars to line up equidistant from the kitchen. It was shaped by the car more thoroughly and more imaginatively than East Coast versions. While the drive-in was not invented in Southern California, it reached a level of refinement there unequaled elsewhere. The Automobile Club of Southern California headquarters was in a dignified Spanish Colonial building, but the real architecture of the car culture was being elegantly defined on the strips.

White Tower, 1936, Camden, New Jersey. At almost the same time that Wayne McAllister's first Streamline drive-in was opened, the East Coast White Tower chain moved out to the roadside from their urban base and found the Streamline style suited to their new locale. Here the tower marked a pedestrian entry; on Simon's the tower was solely a beacon to the wayfaring driver. With its experience with the auto, the West Coast produced a building more imaginatively adapted to the rhythms and needs of the car culture. Here the curved windows and corners were motifs; on Simon's the circular plan was designed to keep the cars near the kitchen for efficient service. Here the lighting was tacked on; at Simon's the neon was integral to the architecture.

McAllister helped develop a workable and influential architectural vocabulary for the commercial strip. Bold block letters outlined in neon, the sculptural use of reflected and exposed neon, the circular pavilions with central mast, the use of glass, and functional elements like overhangs, car arrangements, the visibility of his forms were all highly appropriate, imaginative formal solutions to functional problems. He was well aware of the design world around him through magazines and the works of other Los Angeles architects, and was influenced by them, but his work is not imitative. He was able to transform those sources and apply them usefully in new ways. His strong concepts for roadside architecture were to be remembered and developed further in the California coffee shop and the early McDonald's in the 1950s. Commercial vernacular design developed a respectable architecture that stands in its own right, not simply as a second-rate version of high art design.

The West Coast was still exotic territory in 1940 when architectural historian Henry-Russell Hitchcock toured it to explore the reports of new architecture that filtered back east. He was a distinguished critic, having helped to define the International Style in an influential show at the Museum of Modern Art in New York in 1932.

He must have driven by McAllister's Robert's at Sunset and Cahuenga, and the early Carpenter's down the street at Vine, among others, when he wrote: "Outside Neutra's work and that of his group, most of the interesting things are—so far as I could discover—effectively anonymous. I mean the drive-ins of which there are several good examples on Sunset Boulevard and perhaps the finest of all—despite its unfortunate trademark windmill—at the corner of Glendale and San Fernando. These represent a very model of what exposition or resort architecture ought to be, light, gay, open, well executed and designed to be as effective by night as by day. . . . Nothing in the East compares with the best things of this sort in Los Angeles."

Hitchcock had an insightful eye, despite his failures of research: the Van de Kamp's windmill he refers to was on Fletcher, not Glendale, and was not anonymous, but designed in 1938 by Joseph Feil of Plummer and Feil and expanded by Wayne McAllister in 1940. Commercial architects were probably considered next to anonymous.

A similar route was driven by Philip Marlowe in Raymond

Chandler's *The Little Sister*. Chandler leaves us an offhand description
of the view through Marlowe's windshield: "I drove east on Sunset but
I didn't go home. At La Brea I turned north and swung over to Highland,
out over Cahuenga Pass and down on to Ventura Boulevard, past Studio
City and Sherman Oaks and Encino. There was nothing lonely about
the trip. There never is on that road. . . . I drove on past the gaudy neons
and the false fronts behind them, the sleazy hamburger joints that look
like palaces under the colours, the circular drive-ins as gay as circuses
with the chipper hard-eyed car-hops, the brilliant counters, and the
sweaty greasy kitchens that would have poisoned a toad."

The trip was taken in 1949. It took Marlowe from Mavis Weld's
apartment on Doheny along the Sunset Strip, past Googie's at Crescent
Heights, maybe past Tiny Naylor's under construction at the corner of
La Brea, Coffee Dan's on Hollywood Boulevard, and past two Herbert's
on Ventura, at Laurel Canyon and at Sepulveda.

In almost anyone's mental map of Los Angeles, the drive-ins
of the thirties had become indelible landmarks.

Does Atomic Radiation Promise a Building Revolution?
—*Architectural Forum*, 1954

the '50s

At the corner of Overhill and Slauson, the Wichstand coffee shop stands much as it has since 1957. Through its tilting roof plunges a large slanting dart. It seems frozen in an instant of centrifuge, whirling out of control, forever about to topple. Only the palpable momentum of the space age seems to hold it in place. The Wichstand captured the antigravity architecture of the atomic age.

After the war, America finally got down to the business of building the future.

Wichstand patio, 1957, Armét and Davis, Slauson at Overhill, Los Angeles. Even the strip had sidewalk cafes. The Wichstand's pylon was a separate structure, supported by guy wires, dropped through a hole in the jutting roof.

It was not the utopian future where entire cities would be replaced with identical high-rises and multilevel streets. It was the future the way it would have to come if it were to come at all—piece by piece, paid for by commerce and guided by the consent of the consumer.

By 1950 Americans, and especially Southern Californians, were not finding it difficult to embrace modern architecture. In Europe, the austere white boxes of Bauhaus modernism always seemed to require a religious asceticism on the part of its inhabitants. While influential, it rarely caught on as a widely popular style. In postwar Los Angeles, modern ideas did not require an intellectual devotion or a political vision to be appreciated. The American public had long associated technology with the good life. From the teens, Henry Ford had seen to it that the machine, in the initial guise of the Model T, became a virtual member of the family, lifting burdens and bestowing mobility. Elec-

Arroyo Seco Parkway, *1936, Los Angeles—*
Pasadena. The first freeways were set in parklike
settings.

Freeway intersection, *1950s, Los Angeles. In*
the 1950s, the interchange stacked up to four
levels where the Hollywood, Harbor, Santa Ana,
and Arroyo Seco freeways met.

Mural, Bullock's Wilshire, *1928, Herman*
Sachs, 3050 Wilshire Boulevard, Los Angeles.
The Graf Zeppelin ruled the air between the
world wars.

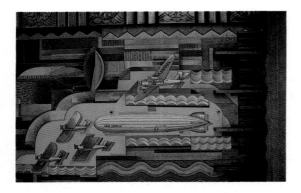

tricity, radios, refrigerators, telephones, household appliances, office machines, and other gadgets constituted an education in modernism for the American middle class under the unknowing auspices of commercial capitalism. The war advanced that education.

Consumer manufacturing slowed during World War II, but the forties did manufacture the raw materials of new styles for the fifties. Technology had made quantum leaps. After the war, factories and inventions developed during the war went in search of consumer markets to keep busy.

The Streamline style had served well as the style of technology before the war, but a new architecture of wonder would now have to be invented. The Arroyo Seco freeway, begun in 1936 and one of the first in the world, was two lanes in each direction from Pasadena to downtown Los Angeles; in the fifties work began on the Los Angeles freeway system with six lanes each way, climbing to multiple-storied cloverleaf interchanges. Bulbous zeppelins promised to rule future transcontinental travel in stately progress during the thirties, but the war had produced the jet plane and the sound barrier was broken in 1947; the jet's civilian application, the Boeing 707 with its rakishly swept wings, offered unbelievably fast travel to all. The 707's gleaming metallic surface, riveted into a smooth skin, dazzled the eye. And even beyond jet travel lay the very possible world of rockets and space travel.

Boeing 707

In the thirties, the primary icon of power was the speeding locomotive, symbolized in Henry Dreyfuss's elegant ballistic sculpture for the engine of the Twentieth Century Limited; only Superman's ultimate strength was greater. In the fifties, atomic energy astonished the world. Science was progressing exponentially, and styles had to keep up.

During the twenties and thirties, Giant Object architecture had reflected the public's sense of wonder and delight about Southern California as a classical Eden, the land of sunshine. But after the war, science was clearly outstripping literary myths as a source of amazing phenomena. The public's interest in fantasy switched gears from oversized fruits, doughnuts, hats, and pets to the power and wonder of atomic energy, television, and space travel. Tomorrowland was an important part of the cosmology of Disneyland when it opened in 1955. The commercial vernacular of the strips documented the change. The future

was a natural theme that the public was ripe to experience, and manufacturers and architects took advantage of that interest by developing a visual vocabulary and products that were associated with the climate of technological optimism.

Plastics were one such product: their moldability and physical properties had made them perfect for the special requirements of electronic gear and plane windshields during the war. In 1945, plastics factories with no war to supply looked to the consumer market. By the mid-fifties the synthetic plastics industry was the fourth largest basic industry in the country, after steel, lumber, and glass.

It was a time of social change, too. The lightweight reputation of the fifties based on hula hoops and Davy Crockett hats overlooks the catalog of new products and ideas that became widely available during those years. These innovations began to weave the social fabric we know today: freeways, television, transistors, computers, station wagons. The fifties brought America Joseph McCarthy, but also Martin Luther King.

New recording techniques, transistor radios, electric guitars, the long-playing record, the creation of the youth mass market all contributed to the growth of rock and roll. The old living room cabinet radio of the thirties was now small enough to fit into a pocket.

The money had started to roll in during the war itself, feeding the car culture on the home front, spearheaded by teenagers. Hot rodding—putting together junk cars because Detroit wasn't making new ones—and customizing became fashions that grew out of the vernacular culture of the car.

The miraculous was becoming commonplace. Technology was erasing seasons, time, and distance. It had won the war. The underlying assumption of the designs is that the world could be brought to perfection and all experience controlled through modern design. The commitment to this ideal was shared in one degree or another by commercial and high art architects alike.

But how were these new materials to be used? What shapes would they take in architecture? Modern theory implied an inherent form for a material or structure based on its nature, but in fact it was not that simple. Plastic, for example, is very plastic; it can be molded to look like carved wood or the inside of a flying saucer.

Futurama Bowl, Stevens Creek Boulevard, San Jose. Bulging and casual, this distinctive lettering was typical in the fifties.

Shapes for styles are not inevitable; they symbolize something the designer is trying to express. With every line he or she draws, a decision is made between possible choices, based on his or her values, or the reflected values of the society. In the fifties, certain sets of lines became associated with the flavor of the times. Two major sources, one mechanical, one organic, influenced these lines.

Hood ornament, *1952 Oldsmobile Rocket 88, General Motors. The swept wings and wingtip nacelles were up to the minute in jet design.*

As the biplanes and ocean liners had inspired Le Corbusier and other modern architects in the teens, the images of rockets and jets seen in newsreels and magazines and models populated the visual landscape of the fifties, giving a particular formal identity to this age. These images played a tremendous role in people's concept of their world and times, and were bound to be reflected in car design and architecture.

The machine assumed a character of benevolence, strength, and progress. Design and architecture represented this aspect of it to the culture at large.

Modernism also admired the elegant structures of organic things, perfectly adapted by evolution to their task, without extraneous ornament.

An issue of *Architectural Forum* (January 1957) foresaw "new forms as graceful as spiderweb suspensions, giant seashells, the branches of trees and soap bubbles," though, it warned, "With so many of the old limits off, nothing will save us from a certain number of highly spectacular freaks, fakes and grotesqueries in the next twenty years."

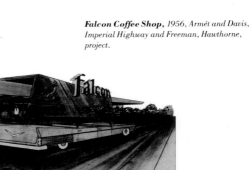

Falcon Coffee Shop, *1956, Armét and Davis, Imperial Highway and Freeman, Hawthorne, project.*

Such organic shapes could be justified rationally but they also softened the strict machine lines of the International Style. Modern architecture had been prophesying just such miraculous fruits from standardization and mass production that would raise the quality of life of the masses. Clean, spare, uncluttered modern design was the proper form of this future, in the opinion of many high art modernists. Classes never before exposed to design in their homes, schools, even factories would be the beneficiaries.

"New, intellectually undeveloped levels of our people are rising from the depths. They are our chief hope," Gropius had announced in 1919, but the masses didn't seem that interested.

Trickle-down theory—high art architects giving the masses what they didn't know they wanted but should have—wasn't working out the way these architects had planned. Instead, commercial architecture was providing much of the housing and public buildings the general public used, but seemed to corrupt modern design in the process. Once taken over by the mass audience, the purity of the style was difficult to control as it was adapted to new situations.

Yet more people came to use and experience modern architecture through the coffee shops in the 1950s than ever visited a building by Gropius. As a result of commercial design's dispersion of modern ideas, a community of common experience and shared vision was created that helped society to grasp the newness and strangeness of the renewed machine age.

Insofar as architecture is a cultural manifestation, the democratization of modern ideas via commercial architecture served an indispensable purpose. The Coffee Shop Modern, however "corrupted," fulfilled the one basic idea of Modernism in the way high art projects remaining on the drawing board or built in a single example could not: the structures were actually used and enjoyed by millions. The facts of the market place that commercial architects understood were often ignored by high art architects; confronting them would be too messy or compromising to a theoretical sense of function. Ironically, the early modernists had founded their revolution on expressing shockingly unadorned functional structures and materials. Expressing the functions of mass-market commerce was a little too radical even for them.

Donly's, 1958, Armét and Davis, 2300 Fletcher Boulevard, Los Angeles. An arrow of glitter stucco balanced on its tip, stabilized by a row of columns along the front.

Norm's, 1954, Armét and Davis, 8511 South Figueroa near Manchester, Los Angeles. Reflected light off the upswept ceiling created a three-dimensional billboard of activity and color: the restaurant was its own advertisement.

God made Southern California—and made it on Purpose.

—Charles Fletcher Lummis

Carolina Pines, Jr. #1, 1955, Armét and Davis, La Brea near Sunset Boulevard, Los Angeles. A canvas canopy over exposed steel trusses sheltered a sidewalk dining area. The canopy's weblike structure contrasted with the strip-scaled signboard with its sprawling letters and the undulating wave of the roof. The three colliding shapes echoed the vitality of the commercial strip.

la in the '50s

Throughout Southern California in the postwar years, business travelers and young families from the new housing tracts of the San Gabriel and San Fernando valleys were lured down the strip by roofs shaped like colossal undulating clouds by day, and by incandescent oases of cleanliness, color, and cheer by night.

The jutting silhouettes of the coffee shops dominated the strip, counterpointing the rhythmic cadence of power lines and speeding cars. At night, by careful intent, these solid volumes transmuted into the nighttime media of light, color, and shadow.

At the corner of Sunset and Vermont, Norm's is a three-dimensional billboard behind gem-clear plate glass to attract the customer's eye. The upswept ceiling reveals a lighted interior of gleaming stainless steel, modern spun-glass light fixtures, and brightly colored decorations. The image of a clean, cheery, modern restaurant is communicated far down the street. Neon pennants overhead, waving in the electronic breeze, spell out Norm's and rhyme with the diamond-shape roof truss.

Los Angeles in the 1950s was a modern city. The opportunities of the postwar boom in the freedom of Los Angeles allowed architects ranging from John Lautner to Richard Neutra full rein in a new phase of Modernism. The optimistic exploration of materials and structures for the new age continued. But as widely publicized as were Lautner's Silvertop, or the series of Case Study houses sponsored by *Arts and Architecture* magazine, or other high art buildings, they were only a

Bradbury Building, 1893, George Wyman, 304 South Broadway, Los Angeles. Los Angeles architecture has long been inspired by futuristic visions. The Bradbury Building offers a Victorian version.

fraction of the architecture that filled tracts and lined commercial strips. The roadside buildings gave anyone driving Los Angeles streets the sense that this was indeed a new era, that the long-promised future of benevolent technology and prosperity had at last arrived to deliver the good life to all.

The future was certainly no stranger to Los Angeles. The Bradbury building (George Wyman, 1893) was inspired by an untrained architect's reading of Edward Bellamy's futuristic *Looking Backwards*. Its soaring interior atrium, topped by a light-collecting glass pyramid and trimmed out in delicate wrought-iron railings and carved wood, gave this vision of the future a curiously Victorian air. Not too many blocks away, the mirrored silos of the Bonaventure Hotel (John Portman, 1976) carry on the tradition of breathtaking interior space and the look of tomorrow, albeit a different tomorrow.

Los Angeles took advantage of its prospering economy, its talent, its burgeoning population, and its laissez-faire tradition to develop an architecture appropriate to the times and the needs of the day. Like modernism's beginnings early in the century, the machine (in Los Angeles, the car) was the inspiration and impetus. The city embraced new possibilities in forms, building types, and materials unhindered by the city plans or stylistic conventions of the past that shackled other cities. A new set of architectural lines was to be called upon to express these changes of attitudes and enthusiasms.

Ralph's Market, Buena Vista at Victory, San Fernando Valley. From Stiles O. Clements's Streamline supermarkets of the thirties to the wingspread of this Ralph's, supermarkets have been seen as a fitting exercise in modern architecture.

The modern landscape was made up of buildings used by a broad section of the public: supermarkets, motels, car dealerships, bowling alleys, car washes, gas stations, stucco box apartment houses, laundries, and coffee shops. Together they offered a panorama of the future stretching to the rims of the Los Angeles basin. Here were the Eichler Home tracts that brought modern outdoor living to all; here were the great linear shopping strips that made every commodity from doughnuts to banking available from your car. There were the great amusement palaces like Dodger Stadium and Marineland and Disneyland with their vast halos of asphalt parking lots, a challenging new architectural element with which no previous generation had to cope. Some buildings, like Sears on Pico and Milliron's on Sepulveda, put their parking on their roofs.

Simpson Buick, Firestone Boulevard, Downey. Many dealers wanted their dealerships to look as up-to-date as their cars.

Man was transforming his habitat dramatically with high-speed bulldozers, scoops, and carriers; entire mountains could be bench cut and turned into a subdivision in a short time.

In 1963, the state and federal governments considered the use of atomic explosions to make an Interstate 40 roadway through the Bristol Mountains outside Los Angeles. This rejected idea was part of Project Plowshare, which was looking for civilian uses for nuclear power.

Bowling alleys, dating from the thirties, became palaces of sport in the fifties, with entries rivaling the portals and triumphal arches of Classical and Renaissance architecture.

Water was as important to a desert city like Los Angeles as its cars, and car washes celebrated it in a way it had only rarely been honored since Bernini's fountain in Piazza Navona. Fountainlike steel pylons sprayed into the sky, melding and pulling apart as the car passed, sculpting space.

Covina Bowl, 1955 P.B. DeRosa, and Austin Daly, 1060 Rimsdale, West Covina. Opening night at bowling alleys and supermarkets were as celebrated as movie premieres. DeRosa was impressed by the prestressed concrete shells of architect Felix Candela, and developed a method with steel and plywood to achieve similar monumental buildings. He was also an admirer of Frank Lloyd Wright.

Car wash, *Third at Edinburgh, Los Angeles.*

The road system itself was an engineered machine, a vast web lacing cities together with banked curves, graded straightaways, service stations to fuel cars, restaurants to rest drivers, and a system of signs and billboards for guidance.

The strip environment was as thoroughly shaped to the requirements of car transportation as the piazzas of Italy responded to the needs of the pedestrian. There, open-air markets and sidewalk cafes were scaled to the walker. The piazza performed many functions, from commercial to religious to governmental, depending on the day or season.

The strip was scaled to the vision of a person in a car traveling at thirty or forty miles per hour with a number of distractions. The car dictated the strip's expansive linear form laid out on the edge of towns, especially in the West, where established block sizes and street widths did not hinder planning. As a result, distances between buildings and the scale of buildings were greater than those in the East.

Holiday Inn, 1956, 980 South Third Street, Memphis, Tennessee. *A broad, bright yellow fascia and a roadside sign constituted the architecture of the original Holiday Inns. Simple and noticeable, they attracted the eye of potential customers on the road.*

The White Towers back East had pioneered the strategy of repetition, which influenced the look of the strip: their buildings all repeated a common castle image that identified the chain in the public mind. McDonald's would use the same technique, as would Holiday Inns, which began in Memphis, Tennessee, in the mid-1950s. The original inns were single story and mostly sign: a six-foot-wide yellow fascia sign with Holiday Inn spelled out in the familiar script was the entire architecture of the building. The roadside sign on even the earliest inns featured a great boomerang arrow and a radiating star; like McDonald's, the sign attracted customers off the highway by its unmistakable physical presence.

Holiday Inn sign, *1956. Star and arrow motifs and script lettering identify this landmark as a fifties product.*

Even religion followed the car culture: the Orange Drive-in Theatre in Garden Grove was the site of one of the inspired moments in vernacular design. It was here that the Reverend Dr. Robert Schuller, following the lead of other ministers in California during the war, first stepped onto the tar-paper roof of the concession stand on Sunday morning, March 27, 1955, to preach to his drive-in congregation. "Worship in the shadow of rising mountains, surrounded by colorful orange groves and tall eucalyptus trees. Worship as you are . . . in the family car."

The landscape of Pop Art was developing. The bright colors, bold delineations, popular symbolism that would inspire Pop artists were being produced by commercial and vernacular processes. This vernacular style was created for recreation, entertainment, and business, but it also had the ability to impress artists (many from damp, overcast England's postwar austerity) with its excess, palm trees, aggressive commercialism, freedom, and crude and vital architecture. The wild forms, glinting surfaces, overscaled hot dogs, clusters of gigantic billboards, private and public fantasies, and neon districts rivaling the most garish sunsets showed a heedless disregard of good taste as it was conventionally known and practiced. Moreover, Los Angeles proved that a city planned on the basis of abandoning most of the rules could work in ways unimagined. The large scale helped create a visually cohesive aesthetic different from but as appropriate as the dense grids of eastern cities.

Thrifty, Santa Monica Boulevard, Santa Monica.

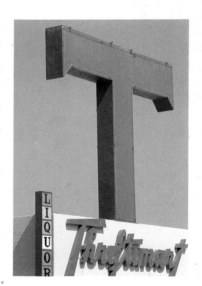

This commercial vernacular is a style of action, of movement, of direction. It is an aesthetic of articulation and contrasts, each element

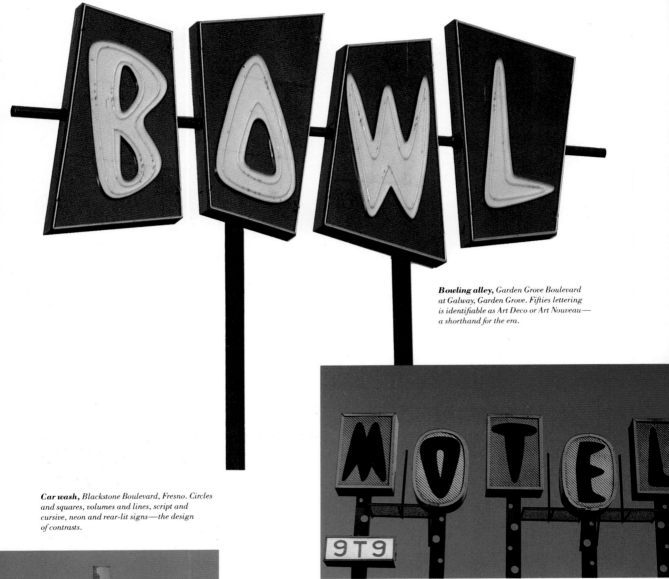

Bowling alley, *Garden Grove Boulevard at Galway, Garden Grove. Fifties lettering is identifiable as Art Deco or Art Nouveau— a shorthand for the era.*

Car wash, *Blackstone Boulevard, Fresno. Circles and squares, volumes and lines, script and cursive, neon and rear-lit signs—the design of contrasts.*

Motel, *Garvey Avenue near Barranca, Covina.*

given its own weight, its own style, its own shape. Disjointed, hanging in midair, combining cursive script with print, its collage design threw together bubbling circles and out-of-whack squares and unexpected angles to pile on all the spontaneity, energy, and tension possible, surrounded by an aura of dingbats (that starburst motif borrowed from printing) and sparkles. Streamlining had glorified efficiency—doing more with less—an appealing idea in the difficult economic conditions of the thirties, but elaboration and even excess suited the abundance of the fifties. Douglas Haskell, editor of *Architectural Forum* in the fifties, equated it with jazz.

Even the names were kinetic: Biff's, Tip's, Ship's, Chip's, Bob's, Norm's, Rae's.

The splayed lines of the Coffee Shop Modern were part of the texture of the fifties. You see the same lines in Elvis's akimbo legs and the hiccoughing, off-balance rhythms of early rock and roll. The metallic echo chambers of Jerry Lee Lewis's voice were as bright and shiny as the neon and stainless steel of the coffee shops.

The car culture was creating interesting architecture in other states, too.

In Texas, which has an early claim on the invention of the drive-in, the Whataburger chain featured a modern A-frame structure.

Oklahoma's Will Rogers turnpike spanned the road at Vinita with a restaurant service area in a parabolic arch, serving both sides with one facility.

Rettig's in Houston by MacKie and Kamrath was a fascinating geometric sculpture in the Wrightian idiom.

White Castle, White Tower, Sonic Burger, Steak and Shake, and other chains in the Midwest and East did not make as dramatic a stylistic leap as their West Coast counterparts, but did abstract and simplify their crenellations into sleeker forms.

The faith had its critics. Lewis Mumford decried "the absurd belief that space and rapid transportation are the chief ingredients of the good life." But the mass audience saw it differently, and, as architectural patrons, proclaimed their belief in the buildings and especially the restaurants they supported.

In Los Angeles other types of buildings used the same popular modern style found on the roadside. The theme building for the Los Angeles International Airport, designed at the end of the decade, featured a circular, flying-saucer-shaped restaurant supported by four tapered landing legs. The Union 76 station at 427 North Crescent Drive in Beverly Hills by Gin Wong of Pereira and Luckman was designed in 1960, originally for the Los Angeles airport where it was to complement the Theme building.

Coffee Shop Modern proved extendable to high-rises as well, with examples in Culver City, Glendale, and Van Nuys taking cues from Wright's Price Tower in Bartlesville, Oklahoma, and Neutra's Hall

White Castle, *Addison at Kedzie, Chicago, Illinois. Commercial vernacular buildings in the Midwest became more abstract and simplified in design in the fifties, but did not open up to the road in the same way as California coffee shops.*

of Records building in downtown Los Angeles.

At the Santa Monica Auditorium, the entry canopy hangs from tapering pylons that rise to extraordinary heights to create a car wash at a civic scale. Even libraries did not escape the car style.

Coffee Shop Modern is also related to Morris Lapidus's New York and Miami hotels and shops, which represented an expressionist, commercial modern style in an urban high-rise context. Victor Lundy in Florida used bold structural expressions in houses, motels, and churches during the fifties. Lapidus and Lundy are only a sample of the architects nationwide that used similar styles. Eero Saarinen's Ingalls Hockey Rink in New Haven (1958) and his TWA terminal at Kennedy Airport (1958) initiated his exploration of curves and expressionistic forms; Skidmore Owings and Merrill's chapel at the Air Force Academy in Colorado (1956), Hugh Stubbin's Congress Hall in Berlin (1957), and Felix Candela's undulating shell roofs were all sufficiently similar to the Coffee Shop Modern to find themselves imitated in the ultimate strip city, Las Vegas. Organic expressionism was not limited to the roadside.

Mearle's, *Mooney Avenue, Visalia. A vernacular version of the drive-in.*

The postwar years in Los Angeles brought a demand for a new type of restaurant, a step above cafeterias and drive-ins in service, a few more steps above diners in cleanliness and family atmosphere, and several steps below the ritzy dinner houses along La Cienega's restaurant row in price. "People began going out more," says Emmett Shipman of Ship's. "They had money they hadn't had before." This restaurant would be distinct from the diner too, a phenomenon largely of the East. Middle class families who may well have had servants before the war now lived more informally. The war had offered better paying jobs to their cooks, so family restaurants were in greater demand.

Drugstore soda fountains at Thrifty's and Rexall had served as hangouts for the predriving-age set. The Ozzie and Harriet malt shop drive-in was a distinct vernacular type.

Entrepreneurs like Bob Wian of Bob's Big Boy, Norman Roybark of Norm's, Matthew Shipman of Ship's, Forrest Smith of Clock's, W. W. (Tiny) Naylor, and Stanley Burke responded with a new type of coffee shop restaurant that followed its customers to the strip: a freestanding building seating customers at counters and tables, sometimes

Romeo's Times Square, 1955, Armét and Davis, Fairfax at Wilshire Boulevard, Los Angeles. Romeo's blinking incandescent lights recalled nostalgically the lights of Times Square. Perforated copper sections were backlit, creating a sparkle effect. Inside, a mural of Times Square overlooked costumed "Juliettes" waiting on tables.

with drive-in service, serving a varied menu at reasonable prices and tapping the twenty-four-hour traveler market. Above all, these restaurants had to be not only accessible by car, but attuned to the subtleties of the car culture and widely appealing.

Good sites became harder to get and more expensive after the war, and the thirties-type drive-in was no longer economically feasible. The competitive pressure led to two solutions: either to larger buildings for greater volume of customers, or to the simplified, streamlined self-service drive-ins devised by the McDonald brothers in San Bernardino and Jack-in-the-Box in San Diego.

Often coffee shops replaced drive-ins: Norm's replaced a Pig Stand at Vermont and Sunset; Romeo's Times Square replaced Simon's at Wilshire and Fairfax.

The style was by no means the only one being used. The same year Honnold designed Tiny Naylor's Paul Williams remodeled a Morgan Walls and Clements Streamline market on Wilshire into a mansard-roofed Perino's restaurant, a high-class traditional image in use for several restuarants and clubs on Sunset Strip since the thirites. That style could have been borrowed for the mass-audience coffee shops.

But the coffee shop entrepreneurs felt the architectural style to be as important to a successful restaurant as a well-designed kitchen. Modernism proved more marketable than snob appeal.

Jack-in-the-Box, Mark II, c. 1958, San Diego, Wayne Williams. The Jack-in-the-Box logo came from the imaginative disguise Robert Peterson and his designers invented for the exhaust fan on the roof of their 1950 Mark I prototype. Designed by Russell Forester, this one-story stand had slanting legs at its sides. Mark II's two-story design was an imaginative circumvention of sign ordinances: by putting four billboards together in a cube, they got the same scale and graphic vitality of a sign in a building. "The towns never caught on," says Peterson. Wayne Williams with partner Whitney Smith was a Los Angeles architect who contributed to the Case Study Houses. The Mark II's graphics were designed by John Whitney.

The quick acceptance of the washer and dryer was under-estimated. . . . (the) rendering of the house showed a helicopter hovering over the flat roof, as if the owner was coming home to the suburbs from his day at the office. His wife is waving to him. Where is she? Hanging out diapers in the drying yard. (The architect's) money was on the wrong machine.

—Esther McCoy, 1984

'50s houses

The vision of the mass produced single-family house has obsessed twentieth century American architecture. By applying the technology of aircraft manufacturing to home building, it was widely assumed by everyone from Buckminster Fuller to *Popular Mechanics* that cheap houses could be built. They would look as sleek as aircraft, too. Combining forces, Monsanto Chemicals, the Massachusetts Institute of Technology, and Walt Disney decided to build a prototype home that in a single leap would shake the public and the professionals out of their reliance on brick, wood, and steel. A new market for plastics would hopefully emerge. It was technology in search of a use. It was the House of the Future.

They decided they were going to use plastics as Plastics, not as mere replacements for wood. They were not going to use two-by-four plastic studs. The Monsanto house designers wanted to explore cantilevers using the strength of plastic and large modular shapes of molded plastic. The house's interior spaces were not exceptional, despite curving plastic walls and modern furnishings. The kitchen-bathroom service core was in the middle and four equal wings cantilevered out for each of the living spaces.

Things appeared and disappeared at the touch of a button. Interior lights came not from a bulb but from glowing ceilings of polarized light. Microwave ovens cooked three foods at once, and ultrasonic dishwashers cleaned the plates. Things that used to sit solidly

Greenbelt House, 1945, Ralph Rapson. One of the Case Study Houses for Arts and Architecture *magazine, a glass-roofed garden brought the parklike setting inside. The decommissioned jeep shows the effect of World War II as the helicopter points to the assumed lifestyle of the future.*

Monsanto House of the Future, 1957,
Richard W. Hamilton and Marvin E. Goody,
Tomorrowland, Disneyland, Anaheim. Four
identical L-shaped plastic pieces made up
each wing.

on the floor now floated, from the island dishwasher and cupboard shelves to ovens that raised and lowered into cabinets.

Swedish modern furniture lived here, not that different from those pieces found in the Case Study houses. The line between avant-garde and futuristic was not easy to draw. Beds were thin urethane pads.

Circular heating and cooling grills decorated the wall. An uneasy balance had to be struck, however, between futuristic convenience and "plain old comfort." A modernistic fireplace devoid of chimney and floating on a flat wall straddled the gap. The many modern conveniences of Armstrong Cork, Kelvinator, American Telephone and Telegraph, Owens-Corning Fiberglas, and Sylvania filled the house.

The list did not include the personal computer. The only gadgets that eventually showed up in the house of the authentic future of the 1980s were pushbutton phones and microwave ovens.

Outside, the House of the Future was a cruciform set on a pedestal, a vestige of an early plan to allow the house to rotate to make best use of solar heat in winter. The cross shape was intended to provide natural light bouncing off the shapely plastic walls of each room and isolate each room from the noise in the others.

The four wings reduced the number of molds required; the house could be made of a few large pieces rather than many small ones, as with a conventional house. Each wing was constructed of four identical L-shaped pieces; a floor was attached to the inside of two, a ceiling to the others. Together they acted as a box girder to create the strong cantilever.

This structure did not qualify as low-cost housing. The plastic alone cost fifteen thousand dollars, when Eichler houses were going for twelve thousand or so with more space. The House of the Future had 1,250 square feet.

The pedestal was painted out so that the white house would appear to float above its Japanesque landscaping. Concrete slabs angled across the surface of a pond surrounded by clipped pine trees and rock gardens.

"Its white, cantilevered wings made cloud reflections in the quiet pool at its base. It looks as though it suited its hillside setting or could fade nicely into a flat plot in the Midwest, or a rocky one in New England, or among the jack pines and live oaks of South Carolina."

Well, maybe, but it certainly looked great between the TWA moon rocket and Snow White's castle.

Living room, *Monsanto House of the Future, 1957, Disneyland.*

Eichler Home, 1955, *Anshen and Allen, Marin County. The Eichler Homes had a greater claim on the title of House of the Future, as they actually made it into the future. The Monsanto house never did.*

Eichler Home, 1955, *Marin County. The casual life style was reflected in the combined kitchen-family room and in the extension of living space to outdoor atriums.*

The modern housing revolution ultimately depended more on mundane technological innovations like power tools, than on helicopters ferrying complete steel-and-plastic houses from factories to building sites. It was the merchant builders who after World War II, relying on management and marketing, economics and financing, came closest

Eichler Home, 1955, *Marin County. Exposed post-and-beam wood structures were the architecture of the house.*

to achieving true mass production in single-family modern housing.

In addition, the Eichler Homes of California brought the indoor-outdoor spaces and structural expression of modern architecture to the mass housing market.

A visit on a balmy Southern California evening to a Granada Hills tract in the north end of the San Fernando Valley shows the vision at its best: craggy shadowed peaks form an exotic desert backdrop against a deepening blue sky. Spread over a small rise, the simple post-and-beam pavilions of twentieth-century man suit the rugged southwestern setting in their way as well as the adobe-and-stone Anasazi communities of Mesa Verde and Chaco Canyon do. Patios create private gardens in the desert for each family. Sheltered by plants, an atrium allows outdoor living even in the heat of the day.

The focus of an Eichler house was on privacy, on the open-air garden atrium at its center; the coffee shop was a pavilion set in the midst of a garden, open to all around.

Inside, partition and cabinet walls rise short of the ceiling, defining living, cooking, and dining areas. With natural-finish wood veneer, up-to-date appliances, and built-in counters and tables, the open kitchen is designed to be seen and to be a part of the living area, carrying over the idea of exhibition cooking from the coffee shop. The broad sweep of the plank ceiling and exposed beams unifies the informal spaces. The bedroom wing, in contrast, is private.

In stretches of the San Fernando Valley, in Marin County, and on the San Francisco peninsula, enclaves of convincingly modern Eichler houses can still be seen carrying the flag of progressive modernism. They are set in a landscape of space-age coffee shops, sweeping cloverleafs, Constructivist car washes, and panoramic supermarkets. Jungle gyms at the playground down the block are fashioned as Saturns and rocket ships.

While Levittown, in the heart of the East, could rely on picket fences and saltbox forms as an easy shorthand for home and tradition, Eichler architects (Anshen and Allen, A. Quincy Jones and Frederick Emmons, and Claude Oakland) helped develop a popular modern vocabulary to communicate the idea of the modern home. In the fifties people not only dreamed of the future, they also lived in its midst.

Eichler Home, *1955, Marin County. The furnishings and accessories of Eichler Homes, including Bertoia chairs, often showed up in the Case Study houses and in the Monsanto House of the Future. The line between Modernism and Futurism was not distinct.*

Mystere, 1955, Ford Motor Company.

Suddenly it's 1960

—Chrysler Corporation slogan, 1957

'50s cars

This was the car you were meant to drive to Ship's.

The Mystere featured black, magenta, tropical rose, and pearlescent white colors with bright- and satin-finish chrome. It was first shown to the public in October 1955.

"It explores an entirely new 'open feeling' in styling, with complete integration of interior and exterior styling," said a Ford press release. The forward half of the bubble canopy, hinged to the hood cowl, could be raised, at the same time opening half doors below the belt line. In true modern form, the distinction between inside and out was obliterated.

Fully air-conditioned, it permitted almost unlimited visibility. The air scoop at the center of the canopy provided fresh air. The rear engine compartment fitted either a regular or a gas-turbine engine.

Detroit's dream cars were a thousand answers in search of a problem. Technology could ease the problems and drudgery of life. But as technology leaped forward, its possibilities sometimes outstripped its practical applications. A General Motors dream car replaced the rearview mirror with closed circuit television.

As walls became windows in modern architecture, so car windows became doors and roofs became windows. Each element was rethought, hopefully for improvement but at least for novelty.

The car of the future underwent the same changes from the thirties to the fifties as had the house of the future.

Studebaker, 1949, Raymond Loewy, designer, Studebaker Corporation. Loewy tried hard to make his car look like an airplane.

The thirties imagined the car of the future in the image of the Streamline. In GM's 1938 Y-job, fenders melted into the hood and trunk deck, but were still distinct, emphasizing the separate functions of wheels, engines, and passenger compartment. Once styling got back on track in the late forties, many companies simply extrapolated thirties forms, creating the bulbous, bathtub shapes like the Hudson and Nash, which had actually been designed during the thirties.

Other car companies cast about for a new direction. Like the coffee shop architects, they were well aware of the advances in technology that portended a new age. Functional or not, the images of planes, jets, and eventually rockets found their way into automobiles, spreading the modern aesthetic.

"It is hard to say whether the car of the future may look more like a raindrop or a spaceship," mused one press release. The spaceship won out.

While Le Corbusier had been fascinated by Spad biplanes, Raymond Loewy's 1949 Studebaker seemed to have engine pods, a fuselage, and a chrome propeller, as well as the famous gun-turret rear window. Advances in techniques for folding sheet metal and molding glass allowed sharper, more sculptural lines.

Advances in paint quality caused grays and browns to be replaced with pastels and primary colors in duotone and tritone paint jobs. The public, just introduced to color television, was developing colorful tastes.

Plastic was introduced first on dream cars and found its way into production in the fiber glass body of the 1953 Corvette. Stylists took advantage of new technologies to see how far they could be stretched. It was Modernism's duty to explore their furthest possibilities.

Leading this exploration were Harley Earl, George Walker, and Virgil Exner, three of the most influential designers of the twentieth century. As heads of styling for General Motors, Ford, and Chrysler respectively during the 1950s, they were responsible for populating the American landscape with over fifty-seven million designed objects. These were not art works hidden away in museums to be visited occasionally by a relatively small percentage of the population. They were kinetic sculptures out on the streets, changing the appearance of America through the aesthetic vision they reflected. Though critics greeted them like chrome brontosaurs, through them as through coffee shop architecture the optimism of technology was made part of the everyday lives of millions of people.

Earl, born in Hollywood in 1893, began his career at his father's coachworks in Los Angeles, designing long and low cars for Tom Mix, Fatty Arbuckle, and other stars. He was always on the lookout for new shapes, and when at an air base during World War II he saw

LeSabre, *1950, General Motors. Harley Earl, chief of styling for General Motors for over thirty years, stands by his baby. A Los Angeles native, he began by designing cars for movie stars in his father's coachworks there. The LeSabre's bumpers, wrap around windshield, fins, and long, low lines influenced styling in the fifties. The headlights, incidentally, were behind the central jet air scoop.*

the Lockheed P-38 with its twin tail booms, the chance encounter knocked auto design in a new direction. Earl transformed the tail boom into the tail fin.

The first fins, on the 1948 Cadillac, were modest, though controversial at the time. In ten years they would grow to phenomenal sizes, traversing the range of images from propeller airplanes to rockets. This change mirrored the leap of the public imagination from conventional air travel to space travel. The fin had a functional excuse: allegedly

Cadillac, *1959, General Motors. Chromed nozzles spitting plastic flame.*

it aided aerodynamic stability, a fairly new science. The principle was true enough. The fact that cars going at legal limits would never create the air dynamics that required such a form was not really important; it simply shifted the design from the realm of technology into the realm of metaphor.

Car stylists added the images of powerful new engines to their design lexicon, and depicted them in the red plastic exhaust flames and chromed nozzles of rear lights. The gaping air intakes of jets found their way into grills. Ford and Thunderbird made a trademark of jet afterburner taillights.

The stylized depiction of flame is common in Asiatic, European, and early American art. Purification, enlightenment, guidance, guilt—the metaphor is flexible. Now Harley Earl added power to the list and made the sculpture available to anyone who saw a '59 Cadillac.

"Even when at rest at the curb, its simple, eye-pleasing lines give the illusion of swift motion," explained GM.

Time magazine called it the "ICBM look." The Olds Rocket, the Olds Cutlass, the Buick LeSabre were all names borrowed from aeronautics.

Cadillac's Dagmar bumpers were called bombs, another ballistic reference, and critics clucked.

"The 1959 Cadillac 'Coupe de Ville' shows the misapplication of the functional forms of jet planes for aesthetic effect," stated one industrial designer, mistaking sculptural metaphor for functioning element.

"They seemed demonstrably effective in capturing public taste," allowed GM head Alfred Sloan, of the fins in his pragmatic view. He gave Earl the backing to continue.

Over at Ford, George Walker, described in a *Time* cover story as "The Cellini of Chrome," admitted he "does not try to design for the conservative few: he aims at . . . the kind of flamboyant luxury he thinks will make every buyer feel like a king of the road."

They found out that sheet metal could be pressed into the shapes of imagination as well as the image of efficiency. And they learned that the public was at very least willing to follow.

General Motors began taking their dream cars on the road in Motoramas, an early form of market research. Appearing in several

Pontiac Firebird, 1956, General Motors. Their greenhouse is a glass bubble, their fuel tank nacelles are in place, their fins are ready for the Bonneville Speedway: the typical postwar family goes for a spin in the wide open landscape of technological optimism.

cities around the country, the company would poll public reaction toward the new cars. A snazzy design would whet the public's appetite for an accessory, a line, a look; by associating that look with the future, the unobtainable, the exotic, they made it desirable when it showed up on the production model a few years later.

The coffee shop architects who began to incorporate advertising and mass-market appeal into their designs paralleled the auto stylists of Detroit in the same period. Within pragmatic engineering and marketing restraints, both still saw themselves as designers. They were trained to have an eye for line and proportion; their philosophical underpinnings were those of Modernism, which required that form grow out of the inherent nature of the material or the production process.

Many of Detroit's stylists from 1945 on have been trained at Art Center School of Design in the Los Angeles area, underscoring the link between Southern California and the car culture.

"California was always a hotbed of auto enthusiasts," says Jim Powers, one of the school's graduates.

The significance of the automobile is not in its elegance as a machine. Technical perfection is an admirable thing, but has not caused the revolutionary transformations in society and culture brought by the automobile. The car's true influence is based on the fact that it is a mass phenomenon. Adopted by most classes in America, its demands influence design and planning in many other fields, including architecture, advertising, marketing, city planning, art, even literature.

You underestimate the seriousness of Googie.

—Douglas Haskell, 1952

the coffee shops

"It starts off on the level like any other building. But suddenly it breaks for the sky. The bright red roof of cellular steel decking suddenly tilts upward as if swung on a hinge, and the whole building goes up with it like a rocket ramp. But there is another building next door. So the flight stops as suddenly as it began.

"It seems to symbolize life today,' sighed the Professor, 'skyward aspiration blocked by Schwab's Pharmacy."

Douglas Haskell, writing in *House and Home* in 1952, was one of the very few editors of an architectural journal to look at Coffee Shop Modern at all seriously.

Haskell had been driving north on Crescent Heights past Sunset with architectural photographer Julius Shulman, when he spied Googie's designed by architect John Lautner.

"Stop the car!" he shouted.

"This is Googie architecture," he announced. Shortly after, Haskell's article with that title appeared in *House and Home*, accompanied by photos of three of Lautner's houses. The term Googie swept through architecture schools and offices nationwide.

Haskell was ambivalent about Googie. He was uncomfortable with what he saw as its excesses. It was modern architecture uninhibited, topping itself each time out. Yet its flamboyance was not just the eye-catching gimmick of a giant hot dog; it had a serious concept. He understood that Googie's free exploration, unhindered by accepted taste,

Googie's, 1949, John Lautner, Sunset Boulevard at Crescent Heights, Los Angeles. The red steel roof gets a running start along the parking lot side before it leaps upward at the street, tethered tenuously by the concrete anchor at the left. Googie's jaunty angles continue to mobilize the animated rhythms of the strip.

Googie's menu. *The exuberant silliness of the name proved irresistible to architecture critics looking for a way to pigeonhole the uppity style of the commercial strip.*

was a necessary part of the advance of design.

Haskell recognized that Googie, far from being arbitrary, had canons of form. It could look organic, but it had to be abstract. "If it looks like a bird, this must be a geometric bird. It's better yet if the house had more than one theme: like an abstract mushroom surmounted by an abstract bird."

Another canon was to ignore gravity altogether: "In Googie whenever possible the building must hang from the sky. Where nature and engineering can't accomplish this, art must help."

A third Googie tenet: "Two or three structural systems mixed together add to the interest of the occasion." Pluralism in all aspects is encouraged; inclusion, not minimalism, is the rule.

Neither was Googie satisfied with sticking to steel, concrete, and glass, the classical materials of Modernism. Taking Modernism at its word, any new technological material should be added to the palette: asbestos, cement, glass block, plastics, plywood.

Even so, Googie had "brought modern architecture down from the mountains and set ordinary clients, ordinary people free.

"Sometimes fantastically good ideas result from uninhibited experiment. Googie accustoms the people to expect strangeness, and makes them the readier for those strange things yet to come which will truly make good sense."

If Haskell had seen a positive side to Googie, the definition quickly lost any subtle shadings and became pejorative. It was a little too commercial, a little too flamboyant, a little too western, and a little too American for serious consideration. In the summer of 1952, Paul Rudolph explained how his architectural education under Gropius had saved him from Googie: "Once principles were seen one could unleash the imagination... without fear of producing 'googie' architecture if the disciplines of the ages were observed."

The term continued to be used through the years, by Haskell again in 1958, by Tom Wolfe in 1969, by Mrs. Walter Gropius in 1975; it maintained its currency. "Googie was used as a synonym for undisciplined design and sloppy workmanship," wrote Esther McCoy in 1976.

The temptingly silly label helped to squelch any serious consideration of vernacular commercial architecture, or Lautner's solid contribution to commercial architecture. Some credit the term with harming his career.

Had it been just another vernacular restaurant, Googie's would not have attracted attention. But it showed the clear concept and careful attention to materials and spaces that Lautner continues to lavish on his buildings. And it showed the individualism and organic design of the American Modernism he had learned from his teacher, Frank Lloyd Wright.

In 1930 Lautner went to Taliesin, Wright's home and studio in Wisconsin, to study with him. He spent most of the decade there, working on large and small Wright projects, including supervising the construction of Herbert Johnson's home, Wingspread, in Racine, Wisconsin. Finally Wright sent Lautner to Los Angeles in the late thirties to supervise the Sturges house in Brentwood. Lautner stayed and set up his own practice.

His very first solo efforts drew praise. On his 1940 tour of the West, Henry-Russell Hitchcock observed that Lautner's work "can unashamedly stand comparison with that of his master." Lautner went to work as a designer for Douglas Honnold, one of the major society architects of the day.

Honnold had no strong design compass, working elegantly in modern and revival styles, but Lautner did, and the houses and restaurants he designed while with Honnold reflect his stamp.

The storefront Coffee Dan's he did with Honnold led to the freestanding Henry's and Googie's, totally integrated architectural designs with the power to delight and shock. Nothing quite like them had appeared on the Los Angeles strip before. At once a part of and transcending their surroundings, they focus in single buildings the shifting, glimpsed lines of the strip perceived from the car. The wit and control of high art were added to the vitality and savvy of popular design. These were the very qualities that made Los Angeles inexplicable from the viewpoint of conventional design. Lautner, with a relentlessly logical talent, knew that mundane commercial and perceptual requirements of a strip site were the raw materials of design. He did not have to mine the past; all he needed was there on the strip. His training with Wright led him to exploit the expressive possibilities in the exigencies of site, program, and structure.

The roots of Coffee Shop architecture are traceable to three Coffee Dan's restaurants that John Lautner designed while working with Douglas Honnold during the early forties.

Lautner's first Coffee Dan's, in downtown Los Angeles, was a narrow storefront that was made to seem wider by applying a thick, rough coat of stucco on one wall. The second restaurant, on Vine near Sunset Boulevard, had an upsloping ceiling that jutted out across the sidewalk to hold the sign; with a floor to ceiling glass sheet and an angled glass entry, Lautner made the facade disappear, uniting inside and outside. At the back of the restaurant, a corrugated glass wall let in light to draw customers from the front. A dropped soffit of horizontal wood strips marked a counter area illuminated by hidden lighting. A copper covered pillar at the front carried light fixtures that threw reflected light against the angled canopy over the front door. Angled counters and booths skillfully divided the rectangular space. Angles went every which way, distinct materials covered every surface. It was a lively restaurant.

The Coffee Dan's restaurants show Lautner's combination of structure, space, and function. To Lautner, human predilection should shape a space, not structural requirements. The cantilevers and bents and concrete shells made possible by modern engineering freed him from having to fit humans into the boxlike rooms of conventional building methods. He selected the vaults and glass walls and trusses and angles of his buildings to fit the original, often unusual, concepts of space he

Coffee Dan's, c. 1942, John Lautner designer with Douglas Honnold, Vine Street near Sunset, Los Angeles, demolished. Lautner set off the skewed canopy outside with lowered soffits and wood textures inside to make a standard storefront space into a lively restaurant.

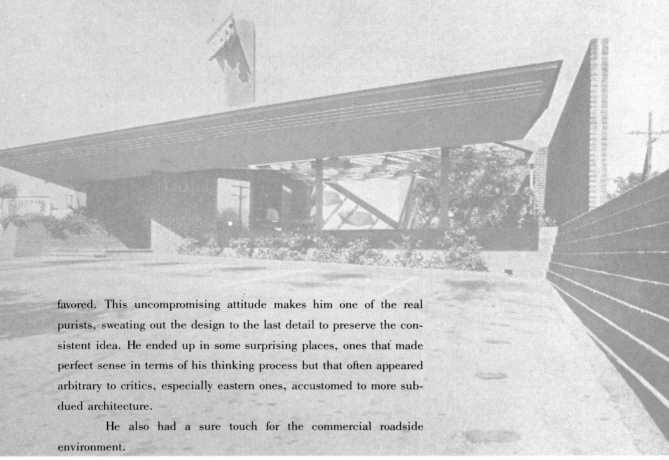

favored. This uncompromising attitude makes him one of the real purists, sweating out the design to the last detail to preserve the consistent idea. He ended up in some surprising places, ones that made perfect sense in terms of his thinking process but that often appeared arbitrary to critics, especially eastern ones, accustomed to more subdued architecture.

He also had a sure touch for the commercial roadside environment.

After leaving Honnold, Lautner designed his first Henry's drive-in at Glendale and Colorado boulevards in Glendale (1947), where all of the basic vocabulary of the Coffee Shop Modern style is seen together for the first time: the eye-catching roof line, the integrated sign pylon, the breaking down of distinctions between indoors and out, the many contrasting modern materials.

Henry's was a remodel of a Carpenter's drive-in. A sweeping prowlike roof protected drive-in customers. At the same time it announced the building visually from far down the street and made the small interior seem larger. It tied the different interior spaces together under a strong line. Low battered concrete planter boxes tied the building to the earth. A garden patio was shaded by light metal trusses carrying perforated copper panels that, when continued indoors, served as lighting fixtures. Each element was articulated structurally, each space defined by a wall, an overhang, a canopy.

Henry's included a dining room, drive-in service, a bar, and a garden for outdoor dining. The forms tied in with the neighboring car dealership on Colorado, also designed by Lautner, where the low battered walls created a raised platform for displaying cars.

Henry's, 1947, Glendale. Perforated metal copper panels floated from the steel trusses creating geometric shadows on the stucco walls. Above, the sign pylon was visible.

Henry's, 1957, John Lautner, Foothill Boulevard, Pomona. For travelers along hot and dusty Route 66, Henry's broad winglike roof, carried by a deep laminated wood spine, created a cool shaded oasis, and they willingly pulled over. It combined a drive-in, coffee shop, and restaurant under one roof.

Lautner designed Googie's restaurant at Sunset and Crescent Heights in 1949, and unknowingly gave an entire range of jazzy modern buildings a name. Googie's red-painted roof of economical structural-steel decking jutted up at the street line, creating a large window that revealed to customers (including a favorably impressed R. M. Schindler) a view of the nearby Hollywood Hills. It also created an elevated place for the sign. A concrete wall anchored the soaring roof.

The concern of restaurant owners for a high turnover rate ran counter to Lautner's intention to create a pleasant environment to encourage lingering. Most restaurants, for example, placed the waiting area near the tables and counters so diners would be aware of someone waiting for their seats.

After Lautner left his firm, Douglas Honnold continued designing dinner-house restaurants like Romanoff's and Eaton's, a prototype for Biff's coffee shops, and a Tiny Naylor's drive-in.

Honnold was well-known in the architectural and social communities for his designs for the homes of movie stars and moguls in Beverly Hills and Malibu. A set designer during the 1930s (as were many other architects, including Stanley Meston) with an elegant sense of line, he could move from style to style with ease and elegance.

The house Honnold designed for Dolores Del Rio and Cedric Gibbons in the early thirties was a cubistic fantasy, but he was just as comfortable in the revival styles of the Hollywood Regency's tasteful, restrained Adamesque proportions and ornament.

Tiny Naylor's, 1949, Douglas Honnold, Sunset Boulevard at La Brea, Los Angeles, demolished. Naylor's was a high-style drive-in by a stylish architect. Its delta wings made it as modern as the latest jet.

W. W. "Tiny" Naylor, who began with a chain of Tiny's Waffle Shops in Northern California, moved south to open Tiny Naylor's drive-in. With its daring winglike canopy and angled strut supports, Honnold's 1949 Tiny Naylor's dominated the busy intersection at La Brea and Sunset like a sleek rocket-plane. Naylor's plane imagery made the first Cadillac fins appearing the previous year, borrowed by GM stylist Harley Earl from the twin boom Lockheed P-38, timid in comparison. Ten years later, they would catch up.

Across the street, Mad Man Muntz's used-car dealership displayed the teardrop tubs of postwar auto design. The sleek lines of Tiny Naylor's were an elegant and modern contrast. Though Kem Weber and Richard Neutra had drive-in projects, Tiny Naylor's was the first drive-in by a prominent architect to be built.

At the same time, Honnold designed the Biff's prototype. The Biff's were part of the Naylor outfit; Biff was Tiny's son. The design was

Biff's prototype, 1950, Douglas Honnold, Hollywood, Panorama City, Santa Monica, West Los Angeles, and elsewhere, remodeled or demolished. With exposed neon tubing, steel channel decking, and glistening metallic reflections, the Biff's seem austerely high tech today. But the horizontal and vertical slabs, pinned together with oblique steel beams, create an elegant composition.

Biff's. *Even with an intermediate planter, the parked cars seemed as much a part of the decor as the exhibition cooking behind the counter.*

a basic glass box of tapered steel I beams and glass infill. Biff's steel-and-glass buildings related to the spare, boxlike pavilions of steel and glass that the Case Study houses of *Arts and Architecture* magazine featured. Both opened their views to the view of Southern California, whether garden or parking lot. The textures of corrugated glass-and-steel decking were used in elegant style. Edgardo Contini, who engineered buildings for Charles Eames and Lautner as well as Honnold, engineered the Biff's.

The Biff's sites took advantage of leftover corners of Union Oil gas stations. It was a small coffee shop with a twenty-four-stool counter and one or two small tables. Cars parked immediately outside the glass walls. A tall rectilinear pylon with the Biff's name faced the traffic. A rectangular canopy of steel decking like Lautner used in Googie's, trimmed underneath in exposed neon, interlocked with the sign pylon to create a nifty Constructivist sculpture.

The Biff's displayed a conscious acceptance of the car landscape. The parked car was practically a part of the architecture. The customers were shoehorned in between the machines that brought them and the machines that cooked their food. Diners and greasy spoons had exposed their grills for a long time, but at Biff's all the kitchen equipment was consciously designed for appearance and function. It was a rational modern look; the structure, the grill, the cooks were all exposed to view. Nothing was hidden. Biff's introduced this strategy known as exhibition cooking as part of the restaurant's architecture and marketing. It was a no-nonsense planning designed down to the last plate receptacle and trash shoot to give a unified, neat, clean appearance.

The cooking grill, for instance, was a raised surface surrounded by a trough for easy cleaning; before this, crevices and corners had allowed grease and food to build up. Drawers were sized for specific pans. Even the cooks were trained to appear and to cook presentably; they were instructed to use fresh pans with butter for each new egg order, so the customer, looking over the cook's shoulder, could see it. Plates were stacked on spring-loaded devices that kept the supply neatly stored but easily accessible. A scraphole for eggshells and the paper on butter pats was provided.

All fixtures were stainless steel, which, though expensive, was used for cleanliness. The shimmering image of silver surfaces was clean and modern. In later coffee shops Formica surfaces, bonded to stainless steel, allowed color and patterns to invade this metallic world.

The design of the coffee shops was often a team effort involving client, fixtures suppliers, and architects. Many of the functional elements that determined architectural features—exhibition cooking, cantilevered counter stools, easy cleaning grills, waiting areas—were suggested by Matthew Shipman, a partner of Tiny Naylor's who was active in the design of the Biff's and later his own Ship's.

Looking clean and neat was a marketing strategy as much as anything, designed to let the customer see the difference between a Biff's and the greasy spoons to which they were accustomed.

Even the food was designed for marketing strategy. Biff's burgers were made of freshly ground meat and served open-faced. It was the modern hamburger, with its functional innards exposed to view to sell the customer on its quality, just as the plate glass opened the restaurant itself to inspection. This is total design, a single theme carried to the smallest detail. The least function could be made an opportunity for design while increasing efficiency and productivity.

The Biff's innovations were widely copied across the country by restaurateurs who came to Los Angeles to see them. Biff's and Tiny Naylor's spread Honnold's reputation in the restaurant business, so that in 1953 when two brothers who ran a small drive-in in San Bernardino wanted a new building, they came to Honnold for the design. But when they showed him a sketch including two giant arches they wanted on the stand, he informed them that if they knew what they wanted already they could design it themselves. So Richard and Maurice McDonald turned instead to Stanley Meston for their design of their hamburger stand.

Coffee Dan's, 1956, Douglas Honnold, Sherman Way, Reseda, remodeled. Square concrete block pillars stitched together by horizontal wood boards with battens create a Wrightian image.

Coffee Dan's, 1950, Douglas Honnold, Wilshire Boulevard, Beverly Hills, remodeled.

Coffee Dan's, c. 1950, Douglas Honnold, Hollywood Boulevard near Highland, Hollywood, remodeled. With a few cues from Lautner's book, this Coffee Dan's opened up the front with centrally pivoting glass louvers.

Bob's Big Boy, 1951, Wayne McAllister, 1000 Colorado Street, Glendale. In 1984, the magnificent sign and the rear-lit Bs gracing the windows were removed to comply with a local sign ordinance.

Honnold's designs for Coffee Dan's in the mid-fifties were even more elegant, essays in Wrightian wood horizontals played off of concrete block anchors, a combination of the Ennis house (Los Angeles, 1924) and the Rose Pauson house (Phoenix, 1940). The same materials shaped into seating areas provided an environment far removed from the cozy, old-timey interiors of today's theme restaurants with comfortable clutters of old milk cans and scythes.

At the back of the Hollywood Boulevard Coffee Dan's, a rear-illuminated mural of plastic created a draw, and helped give a more open feeling. A soda fountain counter at front provided a visual magnet to people walking by. The front window was a screen of pivoting vertical glass sections.

Others worked in the style, too, developing distinctive variations. Wayne McAllister, who had designed so many of the early Streamline drive-ins, moved on to design coffee shops.

When Bob Wian of Bob's Big Boy expanded to several full-scale restaurants in the late forties, McAllister designed them: Most had drive-up service built into the rear of the building. He also designed Hody's restaurant (La Brea and Rodeo, 1948) with Lewis Wilson.

In this period McAllister developed a blockier, abstract style related more to the late moderne forms used in many large Los Angeles architecture firms, than to the structural expression of the Lautner and the Armét and Davis buildings. Large windows were showcases surrounded by striking bezeled frames. Tall rectangular signboards were set against curving horizontal canopy planes in amoeboid and kidney shapes drawn from Abstract Expressionist painting.

McAllister's Toluca Lake Bob's Big Boy (1949) is a magnificent building demonstrating the urban planning possibilities of strip design.

Bob's Big Boy, 1949, Wayne McAllister, Riverside Drive at Alameda, Toluca Lake. The billboard raised to an art form. Its appropriately grand scale helped tie together the vast stretches of western strip space.

In this new car space, traveled and perceived in a new way, wide distances had to pull the jumble together in a cohesive way. A few insertions of the right scale would do it. The Bob's Big Boy sign with its circular great seal was echoed by a circular sign for Lucky's market on a similar signboard farther down the strip. The strip space is spanned and ordered by such moments.

The car imposed a horizontality on the landscape that took on the character of a consistent aesthetic. It wasn't always easy for an eye conditioned by traditional urban forms to see, but it had its own scale, rhythms, and symbols.

Such examples of urban design in the car's landscape are determined for the most part, not by a single design concept, but by a long-running series of decisions, considered and accidental, often in response to bureaucratic considerations of zoning, lot lines, setbacks, or public policy. Yet these decisions create an aesthetic. Thornton Abell, one of the Case Study architects, designed a drive-in for Long Beach in 1945 that was as simplified as his Case Study house. With a simple rectangular billboard perpendicular to the road, a rectangular roof, and plenty of glass, it showed a high art minimalism, but ended up looking very much like the minimal design of straight commercial architects. Mel's drive-ins in Salinas (Butner, Holm, and Waterman, 1950) and elsewhere were almost identical.

It was the prolific firm of Louis Armét and Eldon Davis that established the Coffee Shop Modern as a major popular modern style. Their work for several chains, including Bob's Big Boy and Denny's colonized the style and its image throughout the United States and Canada. But their designs for a number of smaller chains and individual coffee shop operations in Southern California proved the flexibility of the style's vocabulary and their imagination as designers, all while working within the strictures of commercial projects. Enough remain, even altered, so that it is the work of Armét and Davis that creates the major physical memory of the style.

Both were graduates of the School of Architecture at the University of Southern California, Armét in 1939, Davis in 1942. Wright and Neutra were influences there in the thirties. In 1947, Armét and Davis opened an office together after working in the Spaulding and Rex office.

Bob's Big Boy, 1958, Armét and Davis, Garden Grove Boulevard at Gilbert, Garden Grove. Instead of franchising individual units like McDonald's, Bob Wian franchised entire regions to different organizations, resulting in Corey's Big Boy, Kip's Big Boy, Azar's Big Boy, Elias Brothers' Big Boy, Frisch's Big Boy, and others around the country.

Denny's, 1958, Armét and Davis, Van Nuys Boulevard at Sherman Way, Van Nuys. Armét and Davis did a few Danny's before they became Denny's and adopted this prototype style that spread the California coffee shop across the United States. The Denny's were one of the first coffee shops to take advantage of freeway sites. The shift produced another jump in scale, as signs became bigger to be seen from even farther away. Armét and Davis also designed Denny's second prototype, in 1965, with a zigzag shingled roof.

The firm rode the crest of the fifties building boom, designing churches, bowling alleys, schools, supermarkets, country clubs, nurseries, stores, offices, and a few residences, but became known in the field for their coffee shops. They also designed restaurants in oriental, Polynesian, and other themes, but their modern designs were most influential.

"This end of the country was open to ideas," says Davis.

Clock's in Inglewood (1951) for Forrest Smith was Armét and Davis's first coffee shop design. Based on triangles, a span of triangulated windows like a structural truss stretched across the facade, wrapped in a wide-eaved roof. At the entry, a giant red triangular sign in red porcelain-enameled metal was embedded in the building, pointing the way to the coffee shop. They remodeled other Clock's drive-ins and designed a motel in 1955 for Anaheim, which promised to "match in originality the spectacles to be seen in Disneyland," the papers said.

In 1955, Armét and Davis, in association with equipment designer Stan Abrams, designed their first Norm's (8511 South Figueroa at Manchester) for Norm Roybark. This was also their first full-fledged California coffee shop. The bold roof was an elongated diamond shape derived from a structural truss. It was seated on a rough artificial stone wall, its tapering end cantilevered out over the seating and planting. A lightened web steel I beam rose through the roof to carry the sign. A strip of seating edged in glass wrapped around a solid kitchen core at the rear. Space was divided into distinct areas, with angled booths, suggested by Stan Abrams, along an accordian glass wall stretching along the front; at the side, a separate area clustered booths. There was a rear entry from the parking lot. Norm's had semiexhibition cooking:

Clock's, 1951, Armét and Davis, Inglewood, demolished. A bright red porcelain enameled arrow pointed the way into Clock's, Armét and Davis' first coffee shop design.

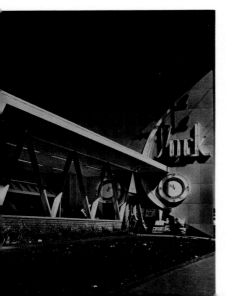

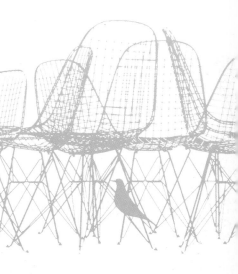

Norm's, 1954, Armét and Davis, 8511 South Figueroa near Manchester, Los Angeles. The first Norm's, designed in collaboration with fixture designer Stan Abrams, featured hourglass and ovoid lights suspended in a space that flowed past flagcrete columns into the burgeoning world of the car strip.

the cooks stood behind a low wall along the counter that hid the grills from view.

Norm Roybark originally wanted a copy of Biff's when he came to Abrams and Armét and Davis. Abrams recommended that he go to semiexhibition cooking for increased production power.

A row of flagcrete columns supported the cantilevered roof at the window line. Glowing white volumes suspended from the upswept ceiling used in combination with indirect lighting reflected against the ceiling provided varied light.

Armét and Davis selected materials that flaunted new shapes and textures. Like Bruce Goff, they would bring a cheap material out of a factory or mechanical use to create a surprisingly beautiful effect. Goff once used goose feathers, oil-derrick parts, coal, and glass cullets; Armét and Davis used refrigeration insulation cork and egg crating for a textured ceiling, and copper foil for fireplace hoods. They had rarely been used for such purposes before, but Modernism drew ideas and materials from unexpected places if it served a purpose. Coffee Shop Modern refused to forget this sort of unexpected invention of early Modernism.

Abrams favored Charles Eames wire shell chairs with fabric covers for the restaurants he designed because they combined a contemporary look with low maintenance. Their legs would not trip waitresses. In his own home, he had Herman Miller and Eames furniture. These chairs became standard in coffee shops, though they were often replaced with fiber glass versions because of wire fatigue over time.

Abrams and Armét and Davis also used George Nelson clocks, plastic and ceramic mural collages and booth dividers by artists like Hans Werner, and Van Keppel Green accessories. These items were the best of modern production design, the same stuff that turned up in Case Study house photos.

Other Norm's by Armét and Davis followed the same themes, but were each individually designed. Roybark once suggested rebuilding every seven years because a new building meant an automatic jump in business.

On the island formed by the confluence of La Tijera, La Cienega, and Centinela boulevards in Inglewood, Pann's multicolored terraced roof hovered with no apparent support over a lush garden of exotic subtropical yuccas and palms. Behind invisible walls of gem-clear plate glass, diners sat in climate-controlled comfort, at once protected from and part of the swirl of traffic around them. An angled pylon holding the neon Pann's sign echoed the lazy lines of the yuccas. Patrons could eat in an indoor patio, a hallmark of the good life.

Romeo's Times Square reversed the typical upswept Armét
and Davis roof by folding downward, but, like Pann's, it sheltered an
interior patio surrounded by a glass curtain wall.

These tentlike pavilions in a desert garden imply a message
about man and nature: with his technology man could overcome the
arid heat and hostility of the natural climate and enjoy the beauty of
nature. The enclosed environmentally controlled interior was a science
fiction dream from H. G. Wells's *Things to Come;* mechanical air conditioning made that dream come true and generally available in public
buildings like fifties coffee shops. This relationship between man and
nature was seen in the imagery of the style.

The lush planted areas of the coffee shops inside and out
make the same point. They function as a visual and aural buffer between
the traffic and diner. They also provide a tie to the natural world in
the midst of the city. This design symbolizes man's dominion over
nature, but also man's need for it.

Coffee Shop Modern balances the dramatic imagery of both
mesozoic nature and twentieth-century technology. Daring cantilever
roofs poise on rough-hewn stone pylons or battered stone walls rising
out of luxuriant vegetation. Spaceage plastic fixtures ornament natural
stone walls.

Taliesin West, 1938, Frank Lloyd Wright, Scottsdale, Arizona. Wright's canted stone and concrete walls holding aloft a modern truss roof created an image of contrasts that Coffee Shop Modern often used.

Romeo's Times Square, 1955, Los Angeles. Armét and Davis renderings (often by Lee Linton) employed exaggerated perspective to emphasize the sweeping modern lines of the design. Though apparently overstated, the building itself conveys the same dynamism in person.

The thread of this concept can be followed back to Frank Lloyd Wright. While many European modernists set modern architecture in sharp contrast to nature, Wright's American attitude toward nature, nurtured in his youth in rural Wisconsin, led him to root man's habitation firmly to the ground, and to build his walls of natural wood, brick, and stone.

At Taliesin West, Wright's home and studio near Scottsdale, Arizona, battered piers of concrete and desert stone created a low visual center of gravity, a stable base settled firmly on the earth to support the light wood-and-canvas canopies that sheltered the indoors. From his earliest buildings, Wright's columns summoned up no memory of classical ornament. Carrying broad eaves extending over the land, they were protective, intended to make man feel at home. They were the very essence of shelter.

Romeo's Times Square mirrored this contrast of stone columns holding aloft a high-tech roof.

The use of such Wrightian motifs was often attacked by critics of the commercial strip, though it was uncertain if they disliked them for imitation or excessive originality.

"The cliches of modern architecture have been incorporated without understanding or discipline into buildings of the most diverse types. . . . We have complete freedom to design whatever we wish, wherever we wish. . . . The result as might be expected is chaos," wrote Mary Mix Foley in *Architectural Forum* (February 1957).

The line between the avant-garde and the futuristic could be a fine one. Tomorrowland, at Disneyland, left a door to the future ajar so the public could peer through before returning to today (or to Fantasyland or Frontierland). Frank Lloyd Wright did not pick his buildings out of a fantasized future, but with his prototypes he did hope to affect the look of tomorrow's architecture.

The line between Wright's vision and Disney's was not distinct in the public mind, however. *Forbidden Planet*, a 1956 MGM science fiction movie starring Walter Pidgeon, Leslie Nielsen, and Robbie the Robot (himself a convincing version of a '48 Buick), needed a "house of tomorrow" for Dr. Morbius's home on a distant desert planet far in the future. The art directors (including Cedric Gibbons, who lived in a Douglas Honnold house) and screenwriters consciously evoked Wright to create a set with that third millenium look. An exposed structure of diagonal concrete and steel supports held its domed roof over a lush oasis. The desert was an image basic to both science fiction and popular futuristic visions. Its wild, unlimited, rigorous expanses were the playing field for man's new technology. With an interior of desert rock walls, encircling floor-to-ceiling windows and terrazzo floors, Dr. Morbius's house also would have made a fair coffee shop.

The coffee shop version of Wright's Modernism was more than a superficial copy. It brought the spaces, imagery, materials, and ideas of Modernism to a broad audience that would never have experienced them otherwise. The style is a major legacy from the ideas and buildings of Frank Lloyd Wright, though artistic autocrat that he was, Wright would have denied it. The ideas were altered for the commercial world as any idea will be when it becomes reality; they were built in Los Angeles, not Wright's ideal Broadacre City. But if they got Wright wrong, they got the Coffee Shop Modern right.

Though clearly commercial in intent, the coffee shops from Lautner to Armét and Davis are convincing as architecture. They are

Tiny Naylor's, *1957, Armét and Davis,*
La Cienega Boulevard near Wilshire, Beverly
Hills. The roof shape is repeated by the sunscreen
on the front and the light fixtures inside. The
solid stone pillars and walls of other designs are
here abstracted into a simple textured screen held
by mosaic pillars at the entry.

advertising billboards, but they are also three-dimensional spaces that work effectively at both street and pedestrian scales. They respond to client needs for a new genre of restaurant in a functional yet imaginative way. They integrate inside and outside in a complex spatial geometry. Their expression of technology is more convincing than that of many early modern works.

They were good architecture because of, not in spite of, their commercialism. "The problem is shifting away from the adaptation of design to machine production toward the highly psychological task of adapting design to an era of popular mass consumption. Once again, the new situation is bringing forth new attitudes, new leaders," wrote Douglas Haskell in 1958.

A new way of looking at architectural design had opened when early modern architects began borrowing from the industrial vernacular world as a source for their own shapes: steel trusses, gantries, water tanks, glass curtain walls, concrete silos each had a different form responding to their use. The classically trained eye read them as a jumble; there was no base, column, and capital here to give an order to the parts. By those standards they were ugly. Yet each form and function was related to the other by the logic of the process—storage to factory floor to fabrication to packing to shipping—which imparted its own logic. The bold vitality of these elements suggested an entire aesthetic. The efficient proportions of a concrete frame replaced the proportions of a Greek order. The rough surface of unfinished concrete became a new texture. Broad unbroken walls of glass united an entire

Dimy's, 1956, Armét and Davis, Pacific Coast Highway, Long Beach. A gantry awaiting the return of the mother ship, Dimy's served in the meantime as a coffee shop.

facade. The rational geometries of steel skeletons created simple boxes and cylinders in place of temple forms and palazzos. The once ugly factory was transformed into an icon of architecture.

Unburdened by the need to meet the standard of taste applied to more respectable buildings, the vernacular could produce buildings of a direct efficiency, a clarifying boldness, a direct articulation, a symbolic content that high art buildings rarely surpass. Commercial vernacular buildings did so just as the industrial vernacular had.

The coffee shop entrepreneur's program required a building that would advertise itself effectively in a hot rod environment. Now the mundane need to advertise a coffee shop led commercial architects to develop strategies with flamboyant forms and plate glass to fulfill and express the function of advertising as the early Modernists had made virtues of the crude functional materials of steel and concrete.

It often started with the highly visible roof; boldly scaled, it was frequently an expression of a new engineering idea, such as a truss, a folded plate structure, a concrete shell.

The sine curve of Carolina Pines, Jr. #1's roof is a variation of a folded plate structure. Similarly, the truss roofs of the early Norm's become supergraphic arrows used as advertising forms. The coffee shop architects "began laying out roofs whose planes, angles, juttings, textures and colors couldn't possibly coincide or blend with anything else around them, and which would dominate the skyline and beckon to a customer," explained a restaurant journal of the day.

The first roadside signs in the teens were ad hoc placards on poles outside a simple shed. Slowly the sign was integrated into the architecture. The impact of this simplification would help a motorist get the message more quickly and easily. Giant Object architecture grabbed the eye and often told you the menu in an instant; the signs of Streamline drive-ins were designed as a part of the architecture.

The signs of coffee shops and car washes of the fifties also echoed the design motifs of the architecture, but went a step further to make the building's roof a sign, too. At night the interior, visible through gem-clear plate glass windows, became a living billboard itself. The angle required to make the interior visible, the scale and illumination of the roof at night, the simplicity of its shape by day were all

Huddle's Cloverfield, 1955, Armét and Davis, Santa Monica. Like the strip itself, the coffee shops had the knack of combining many separate but equal geometric forms in a delicate balance between centrifugal chaos and stable composure. Huddle's combined a prismatic glass enclosure, six separate stick sign poles, a mosaic balcony on the left repeated in stone on the right, and five canvas squares thrown up in the air like a deck of cards.

Carolina Pines, Jr. #1, 1955, Armét and Davis, La Brea near Sunset Boulevard, Los Angeles.

worked out in practice by commercial vernacular designers to suit their needs. If it didn't work, they changed it. If it did work, they repeated it.

The results affected urban planning. The immense scale of the giant angular hourglass signboard on Carolina Pines, Jr. #1 becomes clear when viewed far south on La Brea. It stands out at that distance amid the surrounding strip clutter even today, even after being painted, even after being topped by a standard billboard. Now, though, it is a Copper Penny, and the current lettering gets lost on the sign. Originally, letters of the Carolina Pines, Jr. sprawled across this gargantuan signboard, floated beyond its edge, held aloft in one of those invisible force fields that aided architecture in the 1950s. The Copper Penny lettering that replaced those is tastefully centered and modest in line with recent fashion and sign ordinances. In contrast to the original, these letters are puny, ill-conceived, and ineffectual. The original scale was appropriate to its context; it was urban-scaled art. Current fashion that limits size to reduce clutter is self-defeating. It actually increases the chaotic jumble of the strip by keeping everything to the same monotonous scale. The mix of large and small scale is needed for visual variety.

Pann's sign, listing like an old telephone pole, takes the splayed and angling lines of the surrounding roadsigns and power poles and draws our attention to their patterns and cadence. Through the Pann's

sign, the visual qualities of poles and lines, long the object of expensive civic burial programs as a blight, come to light.

The Holly's sign is offered at several different angles; whatever direction you're coming from, a view is designed for you. It is intended to be seen from all angles at once, a feat approximated by the rapid mental snapshots the eye takes as it scans the landscape through the car windshield.

The signs and extravagant roofs are clearly packaging, but they are also architectural. Their scale and use are a direct product of the commercial demand for visibility and an appealing image, yet they also act as interpreters of their strip setting in elegant and imaginative solutions.

The buildings and signs embrace the icons and communication methods of the mass audience as enthusiastically as the Constructivist designs of early Soviet Russia. The Constructivists worked in a land with a strong tradition of religious iconography used to communicate with a largely illiterate population. This led them, like the commercial architects of Los Angeles later in the century, to explore how signs and speakers and tribunals could be integrated into architecture.

The social commissions of the Constructivists focused on public buildings and social centers for the new man of the socialist age. The coffee shops turned out to be just such centers for the average man. Impromptu business meetings were held over coffee at places like Henry's; different high school cliques took over one or another coffee shop as their hangouts. The coffee shop architects and the Constructivists worked in the service of different gods, of course, but their media were strikingly similar. Boldness, overturned convention, imagination in solving a problem directly were their common themes.

The coffee shops are agitprop for the commercial future. The thrusting lines and unabashed structural gymnastics of the Constructivists symbolized the modern socialist technological era as much as the kinetic diagonals of the Wichstand's pylon. The imagery and the signs are delivered as a three-dimensional architectural experience. A customer first sees the building at the distant scale of the street, where it not only identifies itself but entices customers. Just as the early Modernist Eric Mendelsohn described one of his Berlin office buildings

Dimy's, 1956, Long Beach. *Dimy's delight in exposing its engineering matched the spirit of the Constructivists.*

Ron Dee, *1955, Armét and Davis, San Fernando Valley. The triangular steel box held at a listing angle on its steel beam by guy wires mirrored the dynamic lines and exposed structure in which the Constructivists of Soviet Russia reveled.*

in the early twenties, the coffee shop "is not an indifferent spectator to the whizzing cars and the ebb and flow of traffic, but has become a receptive and contributory element in the movement around it." In Los Angeles this was not mere theory; people conducted their business traveling at fast speeds as a matter of course.

But if the sign and roof are effectively visible at a distance, the building evolves and increases in detail as the customer approaches it by car and then on foot. Everything is designed as part of the whole, down to the ceramic door handle.

The richness of the textures and spaces of the interior are reminiscent of the work of Bruce Goff, another architect influenced by Frank Lloyd Wright. Goff's Ledbetter house (Norman, Oklahoma, 1947) uses many elements that would become popular in Coffee Shop Modern: a broad band of glass stretches across the front; guy wires off masts suspend the porte-cochere; metal is featured contrasting with stone. Inside the elements are seemingly thrown together. Curves and angles go off in unexpected directions without apparent rhyme or reason; they do not follow a conventional grid but in actuality they are shaped by an experiential perception of space. Each form is articulated: the curving ramp, the undulating rough ashlar back wall that disintegrates back into the landscape. A small pool and planting lie under the ramp.

Pann's, *1956, Inglewood. From the sign sized to be seen from a car a block away to the push plates on the glass door, the coffee shops integrated different scales and functions in a sophisticated design.*

Many of the coffee shops use this modern concept of space as well, with curvilinear soffits that move sinuously as one walks under them, echoing the movement. Each element—structure, sign, lighting, furniture, canopy, steps, aisle, wall, equipment, door—is articulated according to its distinct material or discrete function. Even the cooks and stainless-steel kitchen fixtures are exposed as an integral part of the ornament.

An associate of Armét and Davis, Helen Fong, brought a particular concern for human scale, sizing tables, booths, and aisles to make them comfortable to patrons.

Ledbetter house, *1948, Bruce Goff, Norman, Oklahoma. A radial steel truss porte cochere is suspended from masts on the roof.*

Ledbetter house, *1948, Norman, Oklahoma. A serpentine masonry wall forms the back of the house; the front is glass. The detached ramp leads to a second floor.*

Huddle's Cloverfield, *1955, Santa Monica. Soffit, balcony, steps, and light fixture were organized not on a standard grid, but by a kind of choreography of movement in, through, and past each element.*

Pann's, 1956, Inglewood. In the manner of Frank Lloyd Wright, space extended outside past glass walls and around corners, giving the illusion of infinite expansion.

The space of Pann's plan begins in an almost cavelike area with walls of stone, winds along a lowered soffit over the counter, and sweeps up to a high peaked roof and out to the garden like Wright's Unitarian church in Madison, Wisconsin (1947). There are no boxlike corners; visually the space doesn't appear to end as it curves around the end of the counter.

Architecture had been a series of boxlike spaces, with holes punched in walls as doors or windows for communication between rooms or between inside and outside. Cantilevers, concrete-shell structures, and other new building technologies expanded the architect's repertoire of space shapes. Architects no longer needed thick supporting walls at regular intervals. Space could be literally exploded, inside could flow into outside. But along with this freedom came a need for new ways to compose architectural spaces.

Wright began experimenting with new compositions in his

Penguin, 1959, Armét and Davis, Lincoln at Olympic, Santa Monica. Indoor planters, glowing orbs, and original artwork, often in plastic, were integral to many coffee shop designs. Rather than add ornament to the architectural structure, Davis believed in incorporating contemporary art work by artists and crafts people. Then the structure, left simply expressive of its structure, would not date.

early Prairie houses. He would spin rooms off of central cores on pinwheel cross axes. Masses began to balance other masses visually in dynamic tension, not in the mirror image symmetry of the Beaux Arts. Porte-cocheres, terraces, eaves, and planters were flung out into the landscape to claim the surroundings and soften the boundary between inside and out.

Wright and Goff choreographed a flow of movement that carried you along, making you aware of each space and transition. Uninterrupted by conventional doors, walls, corners, or windows, space flows continuously around the next corner and outside. This is the final destruction of the box originally called for by Frank Lloyd Wright. It is also the three-dimensional architecture historian Sigfried Giedion identified with Modernism: buildings perceived as a totality only as one moved through and around them.

Armét and Davis's buildings show how flexible and varied an architectural vocabulary Googie was. While Mies van der Rohe felt that it was not necessary to invent a new architecture every Monday, the coffee shop architects with Goff agreed that it should be reinvented every day.

The curving shell roof could sweep upward, creating a light expansive mood as in Stanley Burke's. Or it could sweep down, creating a more sheltering form in the 1958 Bob's Big Boy prototype.

The style is not a superficial overlay; this is a language adaptable to churches, restaurants, civic buildings, business and professional offices, sports stadia, cars, furniture. It is not undisciplined or arbitrary; it expresses a cohesive modern theory and performs pragmatically in the strip environment.

Bob's Big Boy, 1958, Garden Grove, and *Stanley Burke's,* 1958, Armét and Davis, Van Nuys Boulevard, Van Nuys. The Bob's prototype used a convex roof in the form of a concrete shell, while Stanley Burke's used the same form flipped over. Stanley Burke began around 1940 with a chain of Stan's drive-ins in Sacramento, the San Francisco Bay Area, and Fresno.

Norm's, 1954, Los Angeles. Color, textures, patterns, and light were woven into an inclusivist rather than an austere minimalist aesthetic.

Unlike the progeny of the International Style's glass boxes, Googie did not become boringly repetitive. The proof of the style's success lies not in equaling Frank Lloyd Wright, but in the fact that its vocabulary could be adapted and applied successfully to a variety of buildings.

It did catch on, not so much at the upper echelons of the profession, but among those who build the majority of buildings.

Coffee Shop Modern represented one of the few moments in modern architecture when certifiably modern buildings were also widely popular, though they were condemned by critics as gimmicky hodgepodges. The style, according to a contemporary restaurant journal, was a "reflection of our times in form, color and unusualness, the glass walls are a function of climate and materials. The structural system expresses the environment in its close association with it. The structural system and all that enhances it expresses a purpose (to draw customers); as well as a psychology (subtle appeals to the desire to eat), in an atmosphere which lets the sun inside and then bounces it off harmonized colors and complimentary *[sic]* shapes."

These words are addressed not to the architectural professional but to potential clients in the restaurant business. Yet the arguments are those of modern architecture: that buildings should express their times; that materials and structure should express their inherent natures and functions; that design could be justified rationally; that nature should be integrated into buildings; that technology, e.g., the car, should influence design; and that inside and outside space should flow uninterrupted. The architectural program and especially the imagery demanded by entrepreneur clients coincided with the course of modern architecture in the postwar period.

Perhaps the major monument of Coffee Shop Modern, because of its prominent location on Wilshire Boulevard and because it remained in mint 1958 condition (until demolished in 1984), was Ship's Westwood designed by Martin Stern, Jr. (Chicken Galley addition by Robert Lesser, 1960). It was as if all these modernistic shapes were collected in some wondrous new force field to shelter modern man at the corner of Glendon and Wilshire. Over it all, heading for another planet, was the Ship's sign, a rocket shape chosen to celebrate the newly born space age.

Ship's Westwood, 1958, Martin Stern, Jr., 10877 Wilshire Boulevard at Glendon, Los Angeles. One of the primary monuments of Coffee Shop Modern, Ship's remained in nearly original condition until its demolition in 1984 for a high-rise.

Here the themes of Coffee Shop Modern were laid out in all their vigor: the astounding structure, the car-scaled forms, the glass walls. Classical architecture depicted the force of gravity as it was known then and remained until, at least, 1958. Columns pushed the roof away from the ground and counteracted gravity's downward pull sufficiently to allow safe human habitation. By 1958 supersonic jets, earth-orbiting satellites, and atomic power suggested new forces, new equilibria that surpassed the static forces of gravity. The images of popular architecture delighted in its metaphoric possibilities. So while the pieces of Ship's were, traditionally speaking, a compositional jumble, architecture apparently had been loosed from the need to respond to gravity.

Each component of Ship's was a different form or material, and together they created a dynamic tension; they almost repelled each other. Thin cantilevers and floating curves hovered over solid pillars. The building was multidirectional; sited on a corner, the facades were asymmetrical, shifting as you drove past. On one front face an extruded boomerang shape covered in mosaic tiles impaled itself on the cantilevered truss's spiky ends. Nothing fit together in any conventional order; the visual energy generated was tremendous. It was an exciting, moving, dynamic environment, hurling its occupants into the future as their cars hurled them down the freeway.

Stern says that he wanted to create something distinctive and eye-catching; the butterfly trusses he readily admits were not structural. It was not modern, and not futuristic, just "contemporary," he says.

There was no more worry about having thick walls to keep out the cold or heat; air conditioning controlled the interior climate, and the walls evaporated into gem-clear sheet glass to blur the line between in and out.

The site slopes to the west, so ramps and stairs connected the street level to the restaurant. These were garden paths, meandering through an undergrowth of palms, philodendron, and flowering shrubs. It was a gesture of an oasis of cool and green.

Inside, space flows past the colorful plastics and structural gymnastics into the ornamental yet functional semiexhibition kitchen. The counter stretched at oblique angles to the right and left as you

walked in through the corner entry. Tables lined the windows, a toaster at each one. At one end a dropped soffit and vertical wood battens marked a change in mood. Teardrop and plastic globe lights trimmed the ceiling, their longitudinal sections marked in yellow, red, and white plastic shapes. A screen on one side cordoned off the exit and telephone; its wrought-iron verticals held lozenge-shaped plastic ornaments, some embedded with a chunk of glass, some repeating the rocket Ship's motif with gold leaf and marbles. At the other end a passage led to the 1960 extension called the Chicken Galley. The back wall was a cavelike backdrop of flagcrete, an artificial, rough-textured stone laid up like Roman brick.

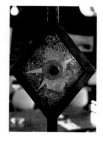

Ship's Westwood, 1958, Los Angeles. Formica, wood, ceramics, and artificial stone and plastics were all used. The enlarged palette of materials created by modern industry opened wide the aesthetic possibilities for Coffee Shop Modern.

The kitchen's stainless-steel counters, the chef's uniforms and hats, the equipment were integrated into the architecture. Low-maintenance terrazzo floors added a pebbled surface to the vertical wood paneling, stainless steel, Formica cabinets, wood-grain Formica counters, blue marbleized Formica ledges, plaid upholstery, random circular ceramic tile, plastic light fixtures, and artificial stone.

Ship's Westwood interior, 1958, Los Angeles. The cooks in their hats and the kitchen fixtures with their Formica and stainless-steel finishes were integrated into the space and decoration of the architecture.

Ship's Westwood, 1958, Los Angeles. The rocket-shaped Ship's emblem was repeated on outdoor signs and menus.

Everything down to the heat registers, coat hooks, and menus were connected to the overall design. The Ship's motif was incised in the glass doors, in neon on the sign, in plastic and gold leaf on the screen decorations, in laminated plastic and paper on the menu, in rear-lit medallions on the exterior.

Martin Stern, Jr. credits Matt Shipman as "instrumental" in the design of Ship's. "He was precise. There was no wasted space."

Shipman was intimately involved with operating his restaurants, and gave details a great deal of thought for improvement. He developed a cantilevered counter stool that would be easier to clean under. He had an operation manual for his managers and employees outlining how they were to behave toward customers.

Ship's Culver City, 1957, Martin Stern, Jr., Overland Avenue, Culver City. The first Ship's.

Influenced by time and motion studies, Shipman tried to streamline the cooking and delivery processes scientifically, just as the McDonald brothers were doing out in San Bernardino at the same time. The turnover at Ship's Westwood reached sixty-seven hundred per day.

Never Closes said the sign out front. Ship's clientele came in tides through the day, from milkmen and bakery-truck drivers before dawn to business people and UCLA students at breakfast, to retired people in midmorning. A general lunchtime crowd carried on into dinnertime, and later came the moviegoers and evening-shift workers and night people. Jetlag sufferers from flights at LAX stopped for whatever their appropriate meal was at any time of the night.

The distinction between high and low art design is not nearly as clear as is usually assumed. Both respond to specific needs and problems, both with varying degrees of imaginativeness and success. Both use the vocabulary or references or aesthetics understandable to their audience. Both rely on an educated taste, though from different cultures of taste.

Carolina Pines, Jr. #2's undulating roof looks like a folded plate structure, but is not in reality; Bob's softly curving roof looks like a concrete shell, but is constructed of steel trusses and stucco to resemble one. In Modernist dogma, such "dishonesty" disqualified a building from serious consideration. In practice, however, many certifiably modern architects took the same license in the search for a technological look: the daringly cantilevered eaves sheltering some Frank Lloyd Wright Prairie houses are (usually) kept from sagging by hidden steel I beams he chose not to express.

When fire codes forced Mies van der Rohe to cover his high-rise steel structure with fireproofing, he felt no compunction about express-

Seagram's Building, 1958, Ludwig Mies van der Rohe and Philip Johnson, Park Avenue, New York,

Mission Hills Bowl, 1957, Martin Stern, Jr., Sepulveda Boulevard, San Fernando Valley. Modern critics accepted the decorative I beams of Mies van der Rohe's buildings, but criticized the "dishonest" structural expression of Googie.

ing the vertical simplicity of the hidden structure with functionless (read ornamental) I beams welded on the outside of the building.

When Eric Mendelsohn could not get concrete to mold the flowing shapes of his Einstein Tower, he built the structure in traditional masonry and covered it in white stucco.

Richard Neutra often painted wood an aluminum color to achieve his modern imagery, causing his apprentices to be tempted to ask him, "What is the best material to build a steel house of?"

Structural metaphor has been a de facto part of Modernism even though its rhetoric denied it in the interests of bolstering its purist rational image.

The messy realities of building do not often allow for theoretical purity. Architecture is an interpretive and expressive art, and artists often rearrange reality in order to get their point across. Perhaps only John Lautner really makes a point of following the logic of a structure to its ultimate, often baroque forms, and he was labeled a Googie architect for his effort. It was easy to dismiss such efforts as arbitrary flamboyance.

Top's, 1956, Armét and Davis, Waikiki, Oahu, Hawaii. Local ordinances would not allow elevated signs, but Top's triangulated sculpture still provided long-distance visibility for the coffee shop.

Alfred Barr outlined the qualities of his candidate for the universal style in 1932: "It requires restraint and discipline, the will to perfect as well as to invent. And this is contrary to the American cult of individualism, whether genuinely romantic, as in the case of Frank Lloyd Wright, or merely the result of the advertising value of a 1932 model."

"The critics bitterly envision a twenty-first century in which the whole countryside will be covered with a combination of 'Usonian Idiot's Delight and automobile graveyard,'" explained one editor in 1958. Usonia was Wright's coinage for his version of the native architecture of the United States.

While the International Style's ostensibly unornamented glass boxes dominated the high art architectural establishment journals and museums, Googie was proving popular. Unlike the International Style, it embraced elaborated forms based on organic patterns and a rich mixture of natural textures rooted in the tradition of American Modernism. The rich floral ornament of Wright's mentor, Louis Sullivan, owes nothing to the idea of minimal expression. In Wright's Southern California buildings, multiple textures crept over his concrete-block structures. It is a rich architecture, throwing a lot of things together in one place. The quest for invention in which American Modernism and the Coffee Shop Modern revelled is not necessarily superficial.

Penguin, 1959, Santa Monica.

Originality, novelty, newness are continuing threads in American culture since the discovery of the New World by Europeans. In their grander phases they caused a continent to be explored and populated as the wonders of the new land were widely advertised. This interest has long been a part of popular culture: the futurism of fifties architecture reflected the tradition of the new. Warnings that this emphasis on novelty would bring civilization to collapse seem unproved after five hundred years. The tendency has been to open up new fields and to welcome new ideas to spread wealth, rights, and possibilities to more and more people. This leads naturally, in a democratic society, to inconsistency, diversity, and pluralism. It tends to move away from the impulse of many modern critics (like Alfred Barr, "appalled by this chaos") to impose an artificial unity of style.

The one certain difference between high art and commercial vernacular architecture was the quality of the rhetoric surrounding it. The high art establishment used talented critics and the established journals to let people know what their buildings were about.

The coffee shops tended to be described in restaurant trade journals as "Chinese Modern architecture."

Part of the bias against the coffee shops responded to their clear lineage from the American Modernism of Wright. Its natural forms and rich textural materials contrasted sharply with the austere modernism of Bauhaus white volumes. But Modernism, despite efforts to force it on to one road, still encompassed a range from Goff to Gropius, from glass-box skyscrapers to coffee shops.

In the first days of Modernism in the early twentieth century, there was no single accepted interpretation of what machine-age buildings should look like. The machine itself is neutral in deciding what it produces, so machine-age architecture proliferated in a multitude of interpretations of what it should properly look like: curvilinear Expressionism in Germany, monumental Futurism in Italy, machine-honed white boxes at the Bauhaus in Germany, the Constructivist erector sets of Russia, the protocubism of the Prairie Style in America. The new age of the machine could mean a lot of things, it seemed. The only link was a freedom that enabled architects to reinvent old elements like walls and windows and play with new techniques. Some of those

Googie's Downtown, *1955, Armét and Davis, Olive at Fifth, Los Angeles. Known for their eye-catching roofs, Armét and Davis could even figure out how to put a fancy roof on a first-floor restaurant in a six-story building.*

threads were cut off, some were slighted as the century passed, but some of them remained nonetheless, supported by a particular audience as the general public supported the organic Coffee Shop Modern.

The commercial nature of the coffee shop did not corrupt the modern design principles that guided its design. Though academic Modernism was never impressed with Coffee Shop Modern and its liberal definition of Modernism, the style fulfills Modernism's aims. The coffee shops are Gropius's dream come true—a new architecture used and appreciated by the masses, expressing the high standard of living brought by advancing technology—except the forms were not what Gropius had anticipated.

Coffee Shop style participated in this modern spirit. It was not a cool, intellectual artistic vision. It was the result of the peculiar influences and transformations that high art ideas undergo when they encounter American popular culture and the commercial processes that turn ideas into realities.

Googie's Downtown, *1955, Los Angeles. The glass walls were as important to see into as they were to see out of.*

McDonald's, 1953, Stanley C. Meston, 10807
Lakewood Boulevard at Florence, Downey. In
virtually original condition, this is the oldest
remaining McDonald's drive-in in America. It
was determined eligible for the National Register
of Historical Places in 1984.

We thought the most practical kind of a building might be a
circular one, but every drive-in looked the same with the cars headed
in all around. We wanted the auto trade, but we wanted something
different.

—Richard McDonald, 1984

mcdonald's

In the 1980s the golden arches are a tasteful electronic signature in McDonald's television commercials, or a low-key plastic sign at a modest height by a McDonald's restaurant. Fading fast into the past is their original incarnation as full 3-D, twenty-five-foot, gleaming metal parabolas vaulting into the sky over the first McDonald's stands. Today's plastic echoes, withered by years of what is called "highway beautification," are mere shadows of those first arches, whose neon trim etched the optimism of the 1950s against the night sky of a thousand suburbs.

Though over one thousand of the original golden-arched stands were built, McDonald's Corporation has been effectively decimating the ranks of early buildings; fewer than a dozen stand in 1985. The old stands become shells and crumble to dust as a new brick-and-shingle McDonald's restaurant rises next door, like the pods arriving from space in *Invasion of the Body Snatchers*. The originals still live as vivid memories in those who consumed the first few billion served.

New and old McDonald's, *Long Beach Boulevard, Compton. The old stands, like the people in* Invasion of the Body Snatchers, *crumble to dust as the new pods are built.*

The first McDonald's hamburger stands were distinctive products of Southern California related to Coffee Shop Modern. Their design's origin is obscured by their proliferation nationwide, but they were designed by a Southern California architect in the region's tradition of fanciful and ultramodern roadside buildings. Like the coffee shops, they were scaled to the commotion and expanses of western roadside strips. The out-of-doors self-service suited the benign, semiarid climate and the mobility of Southern California's post—World War II generation.

McDonald's, 1948, 1398 E Street, San Bernardino, demolished. Maurice and Richard McDonald stand in front of their newly remodeled original stand shortly before it opened with the self-service system McDonald's still follows today.

The earliest of the golden arches were built in the West.

Richard (Dick) and Maurice (Mac) McDonald emigrated from their native Manchester, New Hampshire, in the late 1920s to work as set movers and handymen at motion picture studios in Hollywood. In the early 1930s the brothers went into business for themselves, operating a movie theater in the San Gabriel Valley town of Glendora, east of Los Angeles. Though not highly successful in the midst of the Great Depression, and with no previous experience in the food-service business, in 1937 they also opened a small orange juice stand close to the racetrack in nearby Arcadia. In 1940 they leased a barbecue stand farther east at 1398 North E Street in San Bernardino. The street, a thoroughfare to mountain resorts, cut through a residential area. A high school stood a few blocks away. The existing octagonal building they moved into had screen walls, wide eaves, and indoor and outdoor tables. It was a vernacular version of Simon's.

The stand was popular, but still did little more than break even with the increased competition and costs of the postwar period. Bob Wian, Tiny Naylor, and others had decided to move up to a larger restaurant, the coffee shop, to cope with the changing market. In 1948 the McDonald brothers decided to increase volume by speeding up service, cutting overhead, and honing the food preparation to assembly-line efficiency.

(By way of contrast, in a similar effort to increase volume, Linton's Time Saver Dinettes in Philadelphia [Israel Demchik] used a conveyor belt that brought dishes from the kitchen along the twenty-seven-seat counter. The waitresses, never leaving their stations, waited for the food to come to them. Dirty dishes would return on the lower loop of the conveyor to the dishwashing room.)

"Everybody had the little carhops in the short skirts," remembers Richard McDonald. "A customer would come in, and the carhop would go out, take a menu, go back in, go back out to take the order, go back in and out half a dozen times. Maybe a person only ordered a Coke, so it was a very slow process. My brother and I were thinking there must be a faster way to take an order. Everybody's got carhops. Why don't we do something different?"

With better-paying jobs available since the war, fewer women wanted to work as carhops anyway. The brothers replaced carhop service (itself an innovation to speed service) with walk-up outdoor windows. Customers served themselves at the windows, each of which delivered different items from the simplified menu of hamburgers, french fries, ice cream, and drinks, and then ate in their cars. Customized condiments were eliminated. Paper products and plastic utensils replaced plates, glasses, and silverware, eliminating overhead for dishwashing and breakage. New equipment speeded production. Through experiment and careful food-storage placement, cooking and serving areas were refined to cut labor and time and increase customer turnover. Prices were moderate: fifteen cents for a hamburger (when thirty-five cents was typical), nineteen cents for a cheeseburger, twenty cents for milkshakes, and ten cents for french fries. After a slow start, customers began to come for the low prices, fast service, and absence of tipping.

In the balmy climate of San Bernardino, customers didn't mind lining up at outside windows. Anyway, service was speedy. The number of customers the McDonald brothers could serve in a short time increased dramatically.

"McDonald's went on the theory that if you made it comfortable for the customer and enticed him to stay there with the family, his car took up a space that somebody else could use three times over. So their theory was give them good prices, quality food, and speed. Be courteous to them, but kick them out as soon as you can and make room for the next customer," recalled an early franchisee.

McDonald's, 1954, Stanley C. Meston, 563 East Foothill Boulevard, Azusa, closed February 1984. Neon on the overhead canopy originally pointed out separate windows for hamburgers, drinks, and french fries.

McDonald's, rendering, 1952. With this rendering by Meston's assistant, Charles Fish, the McDonald brothers set out to enlist franchisees for their stand.

The brothers' innovations proved a success. By 1952 they were considering franchising the stands, as other food stands were beginning to do. But before they could change the face of America, they needed a new building specifically designed for their assembly-line operation. The brothers wanted a look that would be clearly identifiable as a McDonald's and as nothing else. It had to be bold enough to grab the attention of drivers day or night along the cluttered commercial strips of Southern California. It also had to include an idea Richard McDonald thought up one night: two giant arches.

They chose architect Stanley Clark Meston of nearby Fontana to design it. Most of his work was designing schools and civic buildings, but he had a good knowledge of drive-ins from his work with Wayne McAllister in the 1930s. Meston had noted how the car shaped the drive-in's plan and scale, and how advertising determined its imagery. But there had been changes in the car culture by 1952; Meston's design was more than a simple extrapolation of the Streamline Moderne. He and the McDonald brothers were to reinterpret the imagery and plan of the 1930s drive-in for the new conditions of the 1950s.

An increasingly sophisticated public was looking for new images of wonder and delight. McDonald's, along with the California coffee shop, were to spread them nationally.

"They walked into my office," recalls Meston. "I'd been recommended and they wanted me to design a drive-in for them. I said we'd be glad to and then we went to work for them."

With that matter-of-fact beginning, an American classic would be born.

The brothers "had this thing all thought out. They had dealt with all the aspects of that operation and they knew what they wanted," recalls Charles Fish, Meston's assistant who worked closely with him on the job.

"It was like designing a factory," says Meston. "I'd go out and observe. There was a production line: the bread was in a certain place, the hamburgers were in a certain place, and then they had a machine to put catsup on. They had to put the pickle on by hand; they never got a machine that would do that. All these things had to be able to go down through a certain succession and they had to work fast." Sizes of counters and placement of equipment took on the logic of efficiency. Like the coffee shops, its attention to its advertising function as a determiner of form, its mass audience, and its adaptation to technology (specifically the auto) made it modern architecture.

The McDonald's prototype is closely related to the Coffee Shop Modern. The bold parabolas of McDonald's arch reflect the same use of simple abstract geometries that Armét and Davis employed in their roofs and bold car-scaled forms, elements that made the coffee shops visible and appealing from down the strip.

Along with their practical knowledge, the McDonald brothers brought Meston a small, rough sketch of two half-circle arches drawn by Richard McDonald. After considering one arch parallel to the front of the building, he had sketched two half-circles on either side of the stand.

Critics have speculated that this prime popular-culture icon, the golden arch, was borrowed from specific models by leading modern architects. Eero Saarinen's widely publicized Gateway Arch of 1948 for St. Louis, Le Corbusier's Palace of the Soviets project of 1931, and

Freyssinet's dirigible hangars of 1916 are cited. The form was also popular among modern architects in Central and South America. A 1932 municipal market by architect Jorge Kalnay created a barrel vault out of seven parabolic arches and it appeared in hotel and office architecture there.

"The people who say things of that sort are crediting the McDonald brothers with a great deal more sophistication than they really had. They didn't get the architectural magazines," says Charles Fish.

Though the final shape of the arches was similar to the high art examples suggested as models, they were reached by different paths. There was no direct influence.

McDonald's, 1954, Azusa.

The arch shape was arbitrarily chosen by businessman Richard McDonald, an untrained designer with no knowledge of erudite architectural precedents. He liked it because it was big enough and different enough to make their small building stand out. The arches were not intended as entries or as structures. He liked the eye-catching quality of drive-ins like Simon's and Herbert's with which he was familiar, though he chose a simpler geometric shape in place of the Streamline Moderne's complex lines. Stanley Meston developed the arch in the popular technologically optimistic design language of the day, an amalgam of futuristic images, kinetic forms, and shiny machine-made surfaces that had spread from engineering, aeronautics, modern art, science fiction, and vernacular design through professional and mass media. The language updated the Streamline Moderne's technological infatuation to a post–World War II context.

The crude half-circles became sophisticated parabolas, with tense springing lines conveying movement and energy. The tapered angles of the flying-wedge roof and the diagonal lines of the windows sharpened the dynamic visual impact of the design. Gleaming surfaces of tile, stainless steel, brightly colored sheet metal, and glass implied cleanliness and machine-made objects. Diagonally set glass reduced glare so that customers could inspect the sanitary food-preparation areas. Beneath the windows and at the rear, streaming bands of shiny red-and-white tile emphasized the horizontals. Glowing red, white, yellow, and green neon trimming the roof, arches, and sign transfigured the solid volumes of day into a glowing dematerialized field of energy

McDonald's, 1953, Downey. Until a city sign ordinance was passed in 1984, the neon flashed.

by night. Night or day, the stand presented a forceful image of ultra-modernity and a distinctive reminder of McDonald's in a design language nearly everyone driving the country's strips would comprehend.

Instead of having a vertical pylon on the roof carrying a sign with the restaurant's name, as did many of the thirties drive-ins, the McDonald's design repeated the arch motif of the building in a third, smaller arch sign at roadside. Speedee, a pudgy character in a chef's hat, strides in animated neon across it. His nickname promoted their service, his placard proclaimed their inexpensiveness.

While being dramatic enough to advertise itself, Meston's design was a simplification and abstraction of the Streamline examples.

"I wanted a simpler geometry," says Stanley Meston. "This had to have all the flair that was justified without getting into what I call rococo. You see that in some models of Cadillacs with flamboyant front ends and elaborate bumpers. I like things simple."

"The whole thing was supposed to be a grabber," says Fish. "The dramatic shapes and this big flaring roof and the high arches were something that would be immediately recognizable."

It didn't look like anything else.

"Do I dare?" Meston asked himself when he looked at the new design. "Is this going to turn out to be some kind of flaky thing, or is this really going to work? Are they going to build this and say, 'This is dumb, how did we ever get around to that?' You go through that moment. Finally I said, 'No, this'll work."

Armed with a drawing of the new design and the convincing success of their own San Bernardino stand, the brothers began seeking franchisees in early 1953. The first ones to bite were Neil Fox, his brother-in-law Roger Williams, and Burdette (Bud) Landon, business associates at General Petroleum Corporation.

McDonald's, 1954, Azusa. Speedee appeared on the brothers' original stand in San Bernardino, and was the chain's emblem until market research in 1962 showed people identified McDonald's more with the arches than Speedee. He was dropped, but in a way was reincarnated five years later when Ronald McDonald arrived. The idea of tabulating the number of burgers sold also began at the first San Bernardino stand, with a thermometer in the window.

*McDonald's 1953, Stanley C. Meston, 909 East
Main Street, Alhambra, demolished. Taken a few
weeks after completion, this photo documents the
original colors and signage of the building.*

Landon recalls: "Neil called me up one day, said, 'What're
you doing? Can you get away?' I said, 'What for?' He said, 'I'm going
in the hamburger business.'

"'Hamburger!' I said, 'You've got to be out of your mind. Will
you make some money out of it?' He said, 'Anywhere from twenty to
one hundred thousand dollars.'

"'For a hamburger stand?'" Landon laughs. "'Well, now I
know you're going crazy.' So that's when the three of us got together
and went up there.

"Dick and Mac had a picture of it. It looked good. It was
different from anything else. If their building in San Bernardino worked,
this had to work. It was so much more modern and easier to run."

None of the three had restaurant experience, so they trained
at the San Bernardino stand for a few weeks. Fox's stand, the first
building with the golden arches to be built, opened in May 1953 at
4050 North Central Avenue at Indian School Road in Phoenix, Arizona.
Using their knowledge developed in selecting locations for General
Petroleum gas stations, Williams and Landon chose a site at 10207
Lakewood Boulevard at Florence in Downey, California, an orchard and
dairy center that had become the home of Rockwell Aviation. It was
the intersection of two crosstown streets on the edge of an orange grove
one mile from the downtown district. They opened August 18, 1953.
The franchise is still owned by Landon and Williams.

"It was an orange grove, and across the street was a nursery
and a gas station," Bud Landon remembers.

"Dick McDonald came down and said, 'You can't build a
McDonald's here,'" recalls Roger Williams. "Dick only saw those orange

groves. Where would all the people come from? We knew what was behind the orange groves. A lot of subdivisions."

The boom was on and Downey was attracting its share of the postwar population.

"This was before the freeway came in. If you went north or south on Lakewood, you almost had to go by it. People on Florence were going to and from work, to and from the store, or to and from the pharmacy, and they were susceptible to stopping."

Williams and Landon paid twenty-five hundred dollars for the franchise rights, not including the building or property.

"Dick said someday they'll charge advertising costs and this and that," recalls Williams. "'You'll never have to pay that because you're the first ones to come in.'"

The distinction of the first McDonald's is often mistakenly given to a stand in Des Plaines, Illinois, which opened in April 1955. But the Downey stand had been thriving for a year and a half by then, and had been joined by several others in California and Arizona.

A third franchise had opened at 12919 Victory Boulevard, North Hollywood, in October 1953, and a fourth, owned by Mrs. Harriet Charleston, opened at 909 East Main Street in Alhambra, California, late in 1953. Other stands opened in February 1954 at 5425 Fruitridge in Sacramento, California, and in September 1954 at 563 East Foothill Boulevard in Azusa, California, and at 1057 East Mission Street in Pomona, California.

During 1954, a Multimix milkshake machine salesman from Chicago named Ray Kroc became impressed that a drive-in in the small town of San Bernardino used eight Multimixers, so he began hanging around the place.

"At that time he was still selling the malt machine," recalls Meston. "He was a salesman. But there were men selling bread and meat and pickles, so he wasn't any standout." After awhile he proposed an idea to Richard and Maurice McDonald: franchising the stands throughout the United States.

Dick and Mac McDonald were skeptical that the self-service idea could succeed in colder, rainier climates. Their thriving business in San Bernardino and franchises operating and planned in the West made them reluctant to risk a national venture. Kroc offered to take the major responsibility for setting up the new franchises elsewhere. The brothers were to receive one-half of one percent of gross sales. They ultimately agreed, requiring Kroc to use Meston's building design and their self-service system.

Kroc's first McDonald's franchise opened at 400 North Lee Avenue in Des Plaines, Illinois, in suburban Chicago, in April 1955. He asked Roger Williams to visit to give advice on how to run it.

The present McDonald's Corporation, founded by Kroc, dates year one from this stand. The stands franchised by the McDonald brothers themselves already in operation were not originally part of Kroc's franchises. McDonald's nationwide success was due largely to the entrepreneurial skill of Ray Kroc in marketing the self-service system developed by brothers Richard and Maurice McDonald.

Even as Kroc began franchising, the brothers continued franchising independently of Kroc with stores in 1955 at 3115 North Blackstone Avenue, Fresno, California, in 1956 at 1900 South Central, Los Angeles, and in 1957 at 981 West Rosecrans, Compton, California, and 3425 Main Street, Riverside, California. They also replaced their original octagonal stand in San Bernardino with a golden-arched unit in 1957. Meston designed only one other drive-in, King's, on Magnolia in Riverside. For it, he shifted the wedge roof ninety degrees and added a crown-shaped sign.

The rest is history. Kroc's story is well documented, but the early days of McDonald's have faded into obscurity, victims of the success that made McDonald's a part of every community. The McDonald brothers' self-service system, efficient food preparation, and Meston's vivid architecture were all developed before Kroc came along. Kroc saw the potential in it and through imaginative marketing and financing spread it across the world.

Kroc began to alter Meston's design, replacing the parabolic arches trimmed in neon with more rounded plastic ones illuminated from within. Basements were added in colder climates. Customer service areas were enclosed with glass. Indoor seating was added later. But it was basically Meston's design that blossomed in over one thousand locations nationwide.

McDonald's, 1953, Downey, and McDonald's, 1964, Rosemead Boulevard, Pico Rivera. The evolution of the arches and the enclosure of the customer service area can be traced in these two shots.

McDonald's, *c. 1978, 5425 Fruitridge,*
Sacramento. This new McDonald's, on the site of
one of the earliest, is typical of the prototype
introduced in 1968.

The frost hit the original orchidlike pavilions in the late 1960s.
The climate of public taste was changing anyway. In 1968 McDonald's
Corporation introduced a new prototype, its low-profile mansard roof
and brick-and-shingle textures a striking contrast to the Meston design.
It reflected a change in public interest to more traditional imagery.
With television carrying the bulk of advertising for McDonald's, the
eye-catching arches weren't needed at roadside to let people know of
McDonald's presence. But the golden arch, taking on a symbolic life
of its own, was retained as a corporate logo.

The arches were born out of the specialized commercial requirements of a car-oriented region to depict an up-to-date vision.
With a change in media, from sheet-metal arches to plastic signs and
electronic pictures of television, the symbol became more traditional.
The ultramodern associations of the sleek arches were lost.

McDonald's, *1954, Azusa.*

Then the archetypal Los Angeles will be our Rome and Las Vegas our Florence. Robert Venturi, 1970

las vegas

Las Vegas must be admired for its devotion to a single aesthetic ideal. Founded in the desert, it was for years a small town, a notch above other southern Nevada towns because of its railroad. Suddenly, after World War II, it began to grow explosively. Even more completely than Los Angeles, Las Vegas was unrestricted by the layered infrastructure of streets, transportation systems, history, stylistic conventions, and industrial, ghetto, downtown, and suburban districts that hemmed in the growth and development of eastern and midwestern cities. To this stage came Wayne McAllister, Douglas Honnold, Martin Stern, Jr., and many other Los Angeles commercial architects. The setting and the architectural problems were similar to those they had dealt with in Los Angeles, and they naturally brought similar solutions.

In this rich soil, the Coffee Shop Modern genus bloomed like a hothouse orchid into uses and sizes unimagined even in Los Angeles. The commercial strip, that uniquely American art form, was raised to its apotheosis. Las Vegas Boulevard South, Highway 91, became known simply as The Strip.

Wayne McAllister's connections with restaurant operators and investors in Southern California helped to sell the idea of the first resort hotel on The Strip, the stretch of highway beyond the control and limits of the city. El Rancho Vegas, which he designed, opened in 1939. Its fifty rooms, around a court and pool, were in a semirustic Old West ranch-house style with shingled roofs, white stucco, split-rail fences,

The Strip, La Vegas, 1963. Las Vegas's Strip raised the car-culture vernacular to a highly evolved state in resorts and casinos and set several generations of towering signs of mythical proportions and shapes against the archetypal western landscape.

Sands Hotel, 1952, Wayne McAllister, The Strip, Las Vegas. McAllister brought the glorified entry and sculptural billboard sign from his coffee shops to Las Vegas.

and a windmill outlined in neon.

The fortunes of Las Vegas accelerated during the war when Bugsy Siegel decided to invest. McAllister was asked to design Siegel's Flamingo Hotel, but he did not accept the offer; coming during wartime shortages, such a building project would not have been able to get the proper materials. It opened in 1946.

McAllister helped design the Desert Inn for Wilbur Clark, who had operated the El Rancho Vegas during the war. It opened in 1950.

The Sands opened in 1952, designed by Wayne McAllister. It was done in the abstract modern style (sometimes called Bermuda Modern in postcard metaphor) of Bob's Big Boy in Toluca Lake. The strong vertical of the sign contrasted with the low horizontal casino and hotel as in the Big Boy. The porte-cochere's angular canopy was suspended from three large-scaled stuccoed bents and dappled with canister lights. A modern colonnade of curved pipe and freestanding block pylons screened the pool area from the front drive. Vertical louvers, marble facing, and bezeled showcase frames ornamented the forms that were angled casually to the curve in The Strip and the driveway loop. Behind the large, low casino space set near The Strip, one or two story wings of motel rooms sprawled out over the acreage. Beyond that was the desert.

Douglas Honnold designed a restaurant and the first low motel wing additions at the rear of the Flamingo Hotel in the late fifties.

Stern was involved with several hotels, both downtown and on The Strip.

Many other hotels reflected the expressionistic modern designs of Felix Candela and Hugh Stubbins that were widely publicized in the fifties. The modern image suited the elegant resort quality that hotel owners hoped would attract high-rolling customers.

La Concha is a fair version of the intersecting hyperbolic paraboloid as used by several Central and South American architects.

Even Bruce Goff designed a hotel for Las Vegas, though it was not built. The Viva Hotel (1960) showed the imaginative range of the style in the hands of a master.

Since the fifties, new imagery has been introduced to Las Vegas—the Roman splendors of Caesar's Palace ("to give it that Greek sense of hospitality," said an executive at its opening), the commercial high-rise slabs of recent towers, not too different from office buildings.

But Las Vegas's coffee shop roots still set the patterns that continue to shape the city. These patterns involved large scales suited to the car, and images to attract customers and mold a strip space. Three of Armet and Davis's Denny's 1958 prototypes with the boomerang roofs more than hold their own on The Strip even today.

The Las Vegas signs remained sculptural, often repeating the symbolic motifs of their hotels: the Flamingo plumage, Caesar's Roman columns and pediment, the Sahara's mosquelike onion dome, the Stardust's starbursts. These symbols, strung out along the disjointed linear stretch, provided the spatial cohesion and architectural order that squares, intersections, and monumental civic buildings did in conventional cities, and coffee shop roofs and integrated signs did in Los Angeles. Today, moving sidewalks arching over vast parking lots, and computerized light displays creating entire building facades continue the tradition of rampant technology established by fifties Modernism.

In Las Vegas, with its single-minded purpose, Coffee Shop Modern developed into an archetypal purity that has fascinated artists and architects. Las Vegas is not an idiosyncratic oddity; its roots are firmly in the pragmatism and imagination of the commercial vernacular forces that mold cities. Its towers of light and moving color put the lie to the common criticism that all strips look alike. It is a uniquely American vision, this oasis in the desert. It is coffee shop heaven.

The Strip, Las Vegas. *Each generation of Las Vegas sign gets incrementally grander. The design strategy for dealing with the distances and competition of the car culture strip was first developed in the California coffee shop.*

Is there another state in the nation, or for that matter another nation, that even approaches California in the quantity, vulgarity and chaos of visual huckstering?

—William Bronson, 1968

'50s critics

Aesthetic judgments have notoriously short shelf lives. Every decade has its respected critics who take pleasure in announcing that the civilized world ended yesterday. A 1918 critic lamented that "Our life is surrounded by ugliness as has been the life perhaps of no other civilized people in any age. The buildings of the Colonial period . . . were often full of charm and dignity. . . . The good architecture came to a sudden end in America about the year 1850. . . . It was the machine which killed beauty. The Neo-Grecque house, of good proportions and dignified detail, gave place in turn to the Victorian or wholly evil dwelling, adorned with lathe work, turned balustrades, little cupolas, scroll gables, incredible gingerbread of every description."

Mirage Motel, *1956*, *Los Angeles.*

" 'Victorian home' is an epithet of opprobrium that is almost universal instead of British in its intimations of gloom, bad taste, and futile showiness," wrote Sheldon Cheney in 1930. "Certainly the high ceilinged rooms overcrowded with bric-a-brac, the false fronts, the iron ornaments, and the rest are eloquent of a period of separation of art from living."

In 1939, the *WPA Guide to California* discussed the "epidemic of the Victorian pestilence." It complimented, though not in so many words, the good taste of the 1906 San Francisco earthquake in destroying so many "Victorian horrors."

The same discerning eyes were turned on Coffee Shop Modern.

"Every new highway built across our land seems to be an

Denny's, 1958, Armét and Davis, Lankershim Boulevard, North Hollywood. Denny's as lush oasis.

Shopping Center, Blackstone Avenue, Fresno. The expanses of the commercial strip are organized by different architectural orders than those of conventional urban cities. Scale, shape, and symbol are used to populate it.

invitation to string out more honky-tonk developments. Too often, new space opened in the cities seems to invite further vulgarity," wrote Peter Blake in *Vogue* at the end of the 1950s.

"It's atrocious design—phony, dated, child oriented trash," wrote William Bronson in 1968.

"The subdivision or contractor-built house, the local store or restaurant, the roadside stand. These are our modern vernacular, the 20th century equivalent of the peasant cottage, the blacksmith shop, the wayside inn," wrote Mary Mix Foley in *Architectural Forum* (February 1957).

"Traditionally, popular buildings—however modest—had an integrity and a dignity which we call beauty. Today integrity is almost entirely lacking.... Until the industrial revolution man never created ugliness.

"It is depressing to contemplate the raucous ugliness which is taking over our land.

"Probably never in the history of the human race has a culture equaled ours in the dreariness and corrupted fantasy of a major part of its building."

Selectively viewing what little historical evidence they gathered, these critics postulated dubious golden ages. In fact, the past had its share of denuded landscapes, cheap boxlike homesteads, commercial clutter, misapplied ornament, and mundane architecture. These aspects were only gilded when critics needed something to contrast with what their taste considered ugly in contemporary design. They ignored the possibilities that the equivalent ordinary and vernacular buildings of today could have the same qualities as the beloved examples from the past.

"Popular taste has become the modern critic's favorite whipping boy," wrote Douglas Haskell in *Architectural Forum* (August 1958).

There was more than a little paternalism in these attempts to mold popular taste to the minimalist taste of the critics. The critics were like missionaries finding immoral the Tahitian natives who did not sit upright for dinner at white-cloth-covered tables.

"In Roadtown the former peasant, cut off from tradition and from his once meaningful way of life, goes a little mad," wrote Mary Mix Foley.

"In its worst forms our popular architecture has become obscene. Furthermore there is an arrogance in this obscenity which strikes the man of taste like a blow in the face. This is a new and particularly 20th century phenomenon. The popular architecture of the preindustrial past was characterized by modesty. It knew and kept its place.

"In our society, at least, it takes a sophisticated taste to be truly simple, and an even more educated palate to achieve richness without monstrosity.... Only an aesthetic counterrevolution by the qualified minority can get us hope for a more rational architecture in the future," continued Foley. The minimalist sensibility tends to exclude those who are messily pluralistic.

Ben's Big Burger, Del Paso Road, Sacramento.

In the thirties, the rise of industrial designers like Raymond Loewy and Norman Bel Geddes had begun to shift the creation of styles out of the hands of arbiters of good taste—East Coast magazines, upper-class society, leading designers, academic critics. Industrial designers sold design by its ability to increase sales. They succeeded, even in the midst of the Great Depression, and design began to be used to mass market cars, appliances, and architecture. They had planted the idea that ordinary objects of everyday life could and should be shaped by aesthetics. They helped democratize design. It was too late to put some limits on what is designed, how it is designed, and who designs it. The head of General Motors, Alfred Sloan, had seen the possibility as surely as Loewy, and had hired Harley Earl to head up what was to become GM's styling department. The means of dispersing taste spread beyond the traditional taste makers.

The right angles, limited palette of materials, and immense glass walls of the minimalist International Style favored by many high art critics were easier to codify into a formula by which buildings could be easily judged. But they did not lead to a popularly successful architecture. It has not yet been proven that such rules are required to maintain or advance civilization, but that hasn't kept successive decades of critics from setting up new indispensable standards of design. Lost is the irony that today's standards were the ones yesterday's were established to prevent civilization from slipping into. Today's tastes are defended as if they are not as transient as yesterday's.

The cluttered jumble of the commercial strip offended the unencumbered neatness of minimalism. Douglas Haskell had been criticized for even talking about it.

Even established architects such as Eero Saarinen, Hugh Stubbins, Edward Durrell Stone, and Minoru Yamasaki were eyed warily when they introduced too many curves or patterns or zoomorphic imagery into their new designs. The flamboyant Frank Lloyd Wright both awed and irritated the architectural profession in the fifties.

The rules of good taste were blinders that caused most architects and critics to ignore the imaginative new architecture of the commercial strip. Still, there were one or two who suspected that this mass-appeal architecture of the strip pointed out a fruitful road for Modernism.

After all, the International Style itself got its shapes and materials from the industrial vernacular, an odd corner of the culture that was supposed to be too ugly to be of value. It is often assumed that commercial architecture could only imitate, not originate.

In fact, the creativity of the solutions of the commercial vernacular often influenced the high art designers. Their directness, practicality, and symbolism impressed many of the creative designers of Southern California, Richard Neutra and R. M. Schindler among them. Neutra saw the bold graphic billboards that lined undeveloped stretches of Los Angeles boulevards in the twenties and thirties, and he lined the cornice of the Universal Pictures Building (1933, Sunset and Vine, Hollywood) with elegant illuminated billboards advertising Universal movies. Schindler's Bethlehem Baptist church (1944, 4900 South Compton, Watts) faces the strip with the broad expanse of a billboard accented by the strip's strong horizontals. Billboards are an unassuming commer-

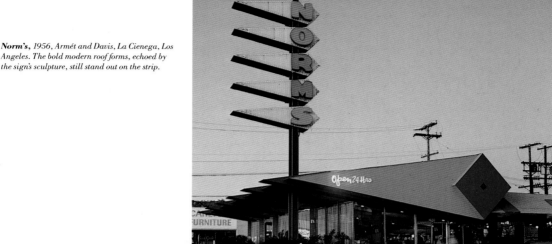

Norm's, 1956, Armét and Davis, La Cienega, Los Angeles. The bold modern roof forms, echoed by the sign's sculpture, still stand out on the strip.

cial-strip device, but Neutra and Schindler were able to see their aesthetic character and transform them into architecture.

Reyner Banham suggests that Neutra's study of commercial vernacular landscape may have been manifested in the distinctive silhouette of the carillon pylons of his Garden Grove drive-in church for that other great exponent of the car culture, the Reverend Dr. Robert Schuller. They stand out as successfully as any of the sky integraters of car washes or coffee shops.

Bruce Goff designed the Venus Soft Drink Bar (1959, Wichita, Kansas), a whirl of obloids and spirals that seemed to float. It was never built.

Other attempts by high art architects to design for the car culture were not as successful. They were rarely built and had no real influence on the direction of actual roadside design. Mies van der Rohe designed a Hiway drive-in in 1948 that, in his universal style, was similar to his design for Crown Hall at Illinois Institute of Technology. The roof plane was suspended below deep steel trusses, and the rest was glass enclosure. The interior was highly visible and the roof was structurally expressive in true Coffee Shop style. The roof, however, was ill-lighted at night and its scale was insufficiently bold for daytime visibility in a proper strip building. It was an elegant work, but did not reflect the functional lessons of commercial vernacular design.

Tiny Naylor's, 1949, Douglas Honnold, La Brea at Sunset, Los Angeles, demolished. With lights glinting in polished metal and chrome, drive-ins were a showcase for the American automobile.

Delighted by a giant cream can stand in California, industrial designer Norman Bel Geddes hoped in 1932 that "we may yet hear of architecture as one of the Seven Lively Arts. It can certainly be made as vivacious as the tabloids, the talkies, or vaudeville."

Henry-Russell Hitchcock praised the same qualities in the drive-in buildings of Los Angeles on his 1940 excursion. "One might hope that the development of a new and widely popular architectural expression waited only upon the development of new functional types, an activity of which Los Angeles seems to be peculiarly adept. . . . For the general establishment of modern architecture depends today almost more upon such commercial work than upon the necessarily limited production of a few conscientious modern architects."

Modern architecture's seriousness (or rather the seriousness of modernists) abdicated that role of providing gaiety and light and a range of symbols to the public landscape.

It continued to be commercial architecture and especially Coffee Shop Modern that filled this role after the war, out of view of most architecture critics.

Slowly a less prejudiced critical eye was turned on the style. Since the early 1950s, J. B. Jackson has been pointing out the vital role the commercial strip plays in a rich, diverse, and everchanging landscape. His influence on most who followed cannot be overestimated. Douglas Haskell wrote about the parallels and possible influences of commercial strip architecture on high art architects in *Architectural Forum* in 1958; he even talked about Disneyland, just three years after it opened; Tom Wolfe wrote about Las Vegas and custom-car design in the early 1960s, and electrographic architecture in the late sixties. Meanwhile, Robert Venturi, Denise Scott Brown, and Steven Izenour took a class of Yale students to Las Vegas in 1968, and produced *Learning from Las Vegas* in 1970, showing that it was all right to look at strip buildings.

Reyner Banham noted the similarities between the coffee shops and the regional work of Neutra and Schindler in his 1971 book, *Los Angeles: The Architecture of Four Ecologies.*

More recently, several books on roadside phenomena, from motels to Giant Object architecture, have been produced, and the Society for Commercial Archaeology has been formed to document and preserve the phenomena.

Until recently, the fifties have been a little too close for critics, writers, and professionals to have a good perspective on them. Most assessments of Coffee Shop Modern are the product of high art critics' low opinion of the fifties: coffee shops are corruptions of the original, pure high art versions of the modern style. In the rush to establish a single reigning modern style, Googie became a dropped thread in the fabric of Modernism. Rediscovered it shows that Modernism has always been wider than the academies acknowledged, that its roots went deeper in the culture than has been admitted since.

The commercial architects of the Coffee Shop Modern architecturally addressed without condescension the aspirations of a broad section of the public. They made the images of the modern good life available to all.

Coffee Dan's menu. *Coffee Dan's, owned by Bunny Bulasky, started in San Francisco and moved to Los Angeles in the twenties, where it became a hangout for theater people.*

We're trying to get away from the old flashy coffee shop look with
its bright, flashy colors, large neon signs and bright interior lighting.
—Owner, White Spot Coffee Shop, Denver, 1973

where are they now?

J

After almost two decades of dominance (a respectable time for any style, high or low art), the style of the coffee shop began to change in the mid-sixties. The late sixties brought a shift in popular taste toward traditional materials and styles using brick, mansard roofs, wood, and shingles. Roadside architecture reflected that change. Instead of grabbing attention, these residentially scaled commercial buildings tried to blend in.

Some restaurants evolved into the Polynesian style; that style's sweeping hooded gables and exposed wood structures were natural outgrowths of the coffee shop style. One of Armét and Davis's associates had traveled to the South Pacific to bring back a trove of tiki statues and ornaments to be used in their tiki restaurants. At some point, commercial architects gave up building the future and began to build the past again. In place of shimmering stainless steel, primary colors, and acres of glass came wide eaves, wood beams, hipped roofs, and plastic stained glass. It was called the warmed up coffee shop in the trade.

Googie's, 1949, John Lautner, Sunset Boulevard at Crescent Heights, Los Angeles. As it appears today.

Even one of the primary proponents of the fifties style repented publicly in words and design: "Armét and Davis admits it was guilty of producing those jazzy structures. . . . (Today) the public is more educated, more receptive to what we architects consider 'valid' design—that is, of the earth, closer to nature," said Eldon Davis in 1973. The future wasn't what it used to be.

The undulating roof of Carolina Pines, Jr. #1 is covered with

McDonald's (now Spot's), 1956, Stanley C. Meston, 1900 South Central at Washington, Los Angeles.

a mansard roof, the outdoor patio is enclosed, and the hourglass signboard has been stripped of its floating lettering. All of the Biff's are remodeled. Henry's in Glendale is demolished, and the Clock's are long gone.

Since the research for this book began, two major monuments, Ship's Westwood and Tiny Naylor's at Sunset and La Brea, have been lost.

Ironically, Naylor's was closed because a stop for a proposed subway in Los Angeles was to be located across the street, raising taxes. The drive-in, icon of the car culture that made Los Angeles, was felled by a subway. You cannot hook a tray for the burger and fries on a window of a subway train.

Of over one thousand of the original McDonald's stands built, fewer than twelve remained nationwide in 1984, and those are going fast. Like the great signs of the Holiday Inns, their physical presence is no longer needed to pull people off the road. Television advertising and computer reservations perform architecture's former functions.

McDonald's (now Star Taco), 1954, Stanley C. Meston, 1057 East Mission, Pomona.

On many prime corners, high-rises have replaced coffee shops, which replaced drive-ins. The very conditions that determined their siting and their form—streets with high-volume traffic that would provide customers to be attracted by the architecture—also determined their destruction when the area increased in density and commercial potential.

Only a glimpse of Googie's controversial roof on Sunset remains, and is probably soon to disappear. Some of the best of the remaining coffee shops are in danger of demolition because of increasing property values. Many interiors have mutated from plastic-and-steel futuramas into Tiffany glass men's clubs.

Still, there are a few survivors, for the moment.

Ship's Culver City, several Norm's, Googie's downtown, and Pann's remain basically unchanged and commercially successful. They were built to last. Romeo's (Johnie's) and the Wichstand still understand the dynamics of the street. Donly's (now Astro's) and Bob's Big Boy in Toluca Lake still punctuate the visual static and centrifugal distances of Western urban space.

In Downey, in the plains of Los Angeles, the oldest remaining McDonald's drive-in still stands as a glinting 1950s time capsule in stainless steel, glass, and neon. In 1984 it was determined eligible for the National Register of Historic Places, a prestigious list of buildings significant in American history. Downey, a quiet backwater in the trendsetting current of Los Angeles, has suddenly leaped into the vanguard of historic preservation.

The McDonald's at Central Avenue and Washington Boulevard is now named Spot's, but with minor alterations it remains very close to its original design. Although altered, the Compton stand, now Nick's Hamburger Factory, is still identifiable as an early McDonald's, as is the Pomona stand.

Today, fifties architecture exists in the limbo that styles inhabit between the times of their initial popularity and their later popular rediscovery. The California coffee shops remind us that Modernism, though on the wane these days, always embraced a wide range of images despite attempts to circumscribe it. Vulnerable to destruction and dismemberment because it is momentarily out of fashion, the coffee shop is as significant a Southern California contribution to architecture as the bungalow, the exotic movie palace, the Zigzag office building, the Streamline market, the Mission house, or the Spanish Colonial anything. Like those, the style forms a substantial body of work, coherent, intentional, successful, and influential.

In the 1980s we can still see and experience the excitement of the 1950s—the prosperity, the optimism, the newness—in the remaining coffee shops and drive-ins.

It is an unfortunate cycle in historic preservation that older architectural styles are only appreciated when they have been out of fashion for a while and most of the best examples have been demolished. Cities have shortsightedly decimated their Victorian, Classical

Pann's, 1956, Armét and Davis, at La Tijera, La Cienega, and Centinela boulevards, Inglewood.

Celestial Motel, 5410 South Vermont, Los Angeles.

twenties. It could be found in plan in accordion windows, or in elevation as a concrete folded plate structure. The pleats stiffened the roof. The Celestial Motel is a vernacular version where the form has become a gesture, a graphic symbol on a stucco box strong enough to convey modernity. It uses three sizes of zigzag in raised and lowered relief. As the Greeks turned wood columns into marble, the vernacular design-ers turned concrete folded plate roofs into plywood. The Orange Julius stand prototype used the folded plate roof.

When the taste turned to shingles and mansards, the zigzags could be trimmed with shingles to form reasonably traditional gable ends.

The concrete shell vault is similar to the folded plate roof.

Carolina Pines, Jr. #2 was not the only building to take advantage of the shape. Oscar Niemeyer had used it in his Church of St. Francis of Assisi at Pampulha, Brazil (1943). Vernacular versions of the shape were seen in car washes, quonset huts, and greenhouses.

This hyperbolic paraboloid shell form produced the space-age lines with which Orbit gasoline wanted itself identified. It also had practical uses: a gas station, where cars were turning and backing, was better off with the fewest number of columns standing around to be hit, so pointy cantilevered canopies, stiffened by their curl, were functional, too.

The structural cantilever was another engineering wonder that allowed for a maximum of shelter and a minimum of columns obstructing

Carolina Pines, Jr. #2, 1962, Armét and Davis, 525 South Vermont near Sixth Street, Los Angeles.

the open space. They were used by John Lautner in his Mauer house (1947). They became a shorthand to announce modernity, evolving ultimately into a pure symbol, the applied bent. Wayne McAllister used them for the drive-in canopy of Bob's Big Boy, Toluca Lake. Martin Stern, Jr. used them at Mission Hills Bowl (1957), adding another motif, steel web lighteners: the circular holes made the central or web portion of the beam more efficient by reducing its weight. They were placed randomly or in line; it gave a designer a chance to add pattern with a functional excuse to an I-beam.

The lightened web motif had been used by the United States Steel Subsidiaries building at the 1939 New York World's Fair (York and Sawyer, with Walter Dorwin Teague).

To a young architect in that period, the diagonal line meant modern. Said one, "Why does glass have to be set vertically? Why can't we slant that glass out and make it look like a railroad train, or whatever?" It showed up in the tilted glass windows of McDonald's and the pilote of Le Corbusier's Unité d'Habitation in Marseilles (1950).

The line was seen in the V-shaped pipe supports of the entry canopy of CBS Television City (Pereira and Luckman, 1952), the Arctic Circle drive-ins, and Gregory Ain's Mar Vista houses in Los Angeles. The supports had a structural excuse, but also added some nice gymnastic diagonals to a rectilinear composition.

Arctic Circle Drive-in, Healdsburg.

Brasilia's heroic assertion of the architect as the maker of the city appealed to architects worldwide, so it is not surprising that these South American modern forms should find their way into commercial and even ecclesiastical designs. Oscar Niemeyer's Brasilia Cathedral (1960), a gaggle of boomerangs, became alternately a car wash, a church sign, and a World's Fair theme building (Space Needle, Seattle, 1962). The pinched waist showed off another of those invisible force fields architecture was utilizing in the fifties, pinching together the structure before it shot off into the cosmos.

The tapering shaft, the needlelike pylon was an insinuating form, elegantly slender, daringly tall, with bursting stars and signs and arrows whirling in orbit around it. Thrust from heaven into earth, it sometimes still gave off flashes of energy from the lightbulbs sparkling on its surface.

Prayer tower, 1965, Frank Wallace, Oral
Roberts University, Tulsa, Oklahoma.

Ship's Westwood, 1958, Martin Stern, Jr.,
10877 Wilshire Boulevard at Glendon, Los
Angeles.

Sven Markelius's Swedish Pavilion in 1939 at the New York World's Fair had a tapered pylon mast similar to Wichstand's, though standing perpendicular to the ground. Another was used in the Prayer Tower at Oral Roberts University (Frank Wallace, 1965). Oral Roberts is an excellent example of how old styles never really die; they continue to have a life of their own outside the professional magazines.

The boomerang was a favorite fifties symbol, from Formica patterns to signs. Its ubiquity caused Tom Wolfe to suggest the name Boomerang Modern for the entire style. It embodied directionality and movement, but also had the indeterminate shape of an energy field. It could be extruded, as at Ship's, act as a modern version of the old-fashioned arrow for a sign, or line itself up in an ultramodern colonnade.

It had many variations: the amoeboid, the kidney shape, the artist's palette, the biomorphic squiggles of Joan Miro and Jean Arp. Isamu Noguchi may have designed the first kidney-shaped pool in Los Angeles in 1935 for the Joseph von Sternberg house by Richard Neutra. The difficulty of pinning down the identity and source of the shape points to its wide acceptance as a shorthand for the modern throughout the culture.

The boomerang lives on into New Wave and Heavy Metal in the Gibson Flying V guitars.

The dingbat, the starburst, the sputnik, the frozen sparkler are all descriptions for a symbol widely used in signs and ornaments in the fifties. It depicted energy caught in the act of explosive release, like a corruscating diamond. The space imagery inherent in the shape

Pic Wood Theater, originally by S. Charles Lee,
Pico at Westwood, Los Angeles.

Bowling Alley, *Pico near Third, Santa Monica.*

reflected the optimism of an age that topped itself by going from amazing feat to unparalleled wonder.

An earlier version of this spiky ball was seen at the 1939 New York World's Fair. It was used to depict electricity in the Star Pylon by architects Francis Keally and Leonard Dean.

The spiky ball was a variation on the atomic symbol, four electrons in a symmetric orbit around a nucleus. Spencer Weart's research has revealed that Neils Bohr first used the symbol as a diagram of the atom in 1912. It was commonly used in scientific journals, but caught on popularly after World War II when atomic energy was suddenly center stage, though it was no longer considered an accurate depiction of the atom. Like the sputnik shape, it contrasted a solid volume with the pure geometry of lines. The same aesthetic concept was seen in some Eames chairs, which contrasted molded plywood planes with thin metal legs. George Nelson designed wall clocks in the starburst shape in the late forties, which showed up in many homes.

Car Dealership, *1959, Melvin Zeitvogel, El Cajon at 34th Street, San Diego.*

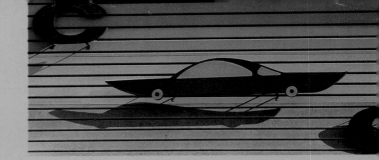

Car wash, *Pico at Sepulveda, Los Angeles.*

I ask not for the great, the remote, the romantic. . . . I embrace the common, I explore and sit at the feet of the familiar, the low.

Ralph Waldo Emerson, 1837

guided tour of googie

Chrysler Flightsweep, c. 1955.

Touring is the only serious way to understand the western commercial strip. A photo freezes a single view, but the true experience of these buildings includes the drive to get there, the surprising juxtapositions you run across on the way, and the rhythmic stretches of endless boulevard that become a form of meditation.

This is an eclectic though not exhaustive list, ranging from the most baroque car washes and coffee shops to simple vernacular versions of fifties motifs and a few selections where high art architects may have been influenced by the roadside. Addresses are noted as closely as possible, but there is no guarantee that buildings will still be in their original state when you get there. Several that have been remodeled are noted where some fragments of the original are still visible, at least to commercial archaeologists. Prototypes used by chains are noted.

Though this list focuses on the Los Angeles area, other cities have excellent strips, too: Las Vegas, Blackstone Boulevard in Fresno, Business route 66 through Albuquerque, Virginia Street in Reno. Business routes, the old highways through the center of smaller towns like Barstow, Visalia, and Merced, can be rewarding.

LOS ANGELES: WEST SIDE

Biff's (now Ace Music), 1714 Wilshire near Seventeenth, Santa Monica (rem.) (chain).

Coffee Dan's (now Biff's), Wilshire at Second, Santa Monica, 1954, Douglas Honnold (rem.).

Bowl, 234 Pico at Third, Santa Monica.

Santa Monica Civic Auditorium, Main at Pico, Santa Monica.

Penguin, Lincoln at Olympic, Santa Monica, 1959, Armét and Davis.

Car wash, Ocean Park at Lincoln, Santa Monica (chain).

Library, 1704 Montana Avenue, Santa Monica.

Rae's, 2901 Pico Boulevard, Santa Monica, 1952, A. L. Collins.

Thrifty, Santa Monica near Bundy, West Los Angeles (chain).

Biff's (now camera store), 10811 Pico at Westwood, West Los Angeles, 1950, Douglas Honnold (rem.) (chain).

Union 76 Gas Station, 427 North Crescent Drive, Beverly Hills, 1965, Pereira and Luckman, Gin Wong designer.

Car wash, Pico at Beverly Glen, Century City (chain).

Ship's Culver City, Overland at Washington, Culver City, 1957.

Memorial Hospital Medical Center, Venice Boulevard, Culver City.

Car wash, Venice Boulevard, Culver City (chain).

Apartment, LaSalle at Culver, Culver City.

Norm's, Washington at La Cienega, Los Angeles, Armét and Davis (rem.).

Baldwin Theater, La Brea at Coliseum, Baldwin Hills, 1949, Lewis Wilson (rem.).

Broadway Department Store, Crenshaw at Santa Barbara, Los Angeles, 1949, Albert Gardner.

May Company, Crenshaw at Santa Barbara, Los Angeles, 1948, A. C. Martin.

LOS ANGELES: CENTRAL WILSHIRE

Romeo's Times Square (now Johnie's), Wilshire at Fairfax, 1955, Armét and Davis (rem.).

CBS Television City, 7800 Beverly at Fairfax, 1952, Pereira and Luckman.

Car wash, Third near Crescent Heights (chain).

Ship's La Cienega, La Cienega at Olympic, 1963, Armét and Davis.

Tiny Naylor's (now Beverly Hills Cafe), La Cienega north of Wilshire, 1957, Armét and Davis.

Norm's, La Cienega near Melrose, 1957, Armét and Davis.

Sears Roebuck and Company, Pico at West, 1939, Reddon and Raben.

LOS ANGELES: EAST WILSHIRE

Carolina Pines, Jr. #2 (now Jerry's), 525 South Vermont Avenue near Sixth, 1962, Armét and Davis.

Robert Taylor Carwash, Rampart at Sixth (chain).

Tiny Naylor's, 3037 Wilshire Boulevard (rem.).

LOS ANGELES: HOLLYWOOD

Ben Frank's, Sunset Strip, 1962, Lane and Schlick.

Googie's, Sunset at Crescent Heights, 1949, John Lautner (rem.).

Schwab's Drugstore, Sunset at Crescent Heights, Armét and Davis.

Screen Actor's Guild, 7750 West Sunset Boulevard.

Pioneer Chicken, 7290 West Sunset Boulevard, 1965 (chain).

Ralph's Market, 7257 West Sunset Boulevard.

Carolina Pines, Jr. #1 (now Copper Penny), La Brea north of Sunset, 1955, Armét and Davis (rem.).

Carolina Pines Motel (now Stardust), La Brea north of sunset, 1960, Armét and Davis (rem.).

Hallmark Motel, 7023 Sunset Boulevard.

Gas station, Melrose near Fuller (chain).

Pontiac dealership, La Brea near Third.

Irv White Buick Dealership, La Brea near Third.

Car wash, La Brea at DeLongpre (chain).

Car wash, Highland at Sunset (chain).

ABC Studio, Vine north of Sunset.

Nickodell's, 5511 Melrose Boulevard.

Pioneer Chicken, 1716 North Western north of Hollywood, 1963 (chain).

Norm's, Vermont at Sunset, 1957, Armét and Davis.

Smorgyburger (now International House of Pancakes), 1027 Vermont south of Santa Monica (chain).

Sherri's 5465 Santa Monica east of Vermont, 1962, Guy Bartoli.

Donly's (now Astro's), 2300 Fletcher Boulevard, Silver Lake, 1958, Armét and Davis.

LOS ANGELES: DOWNTOWN

Googie's, Olive at Fifth, 1955, Armét and Davis.

Dodger Stadium, Elysian Park.

Coliseum French Dip, King at Figueroa.

Hot dog stand, Olympic at Central.

McDonald's (now Stop's), 1900 South Central at Washington, 1956, Stanley C. Meston (chain).

INGLEWOOD, HAWTHORNE, GARDENA

Wichstand, Slauson at Overhill, Inglewood, 1957, Armét and Davis.

Pann's, at La Tijera, La Cienega and Centinela boulevards, Inglewood, 1955, Armét and Davis.

Jump N' Jack, Slauson at Overhill, Inglewood, 1952, Armét and Davis.

Teddy's, Slauson near Crenshaw, Los Angeles, Armét and Davis (rem.).

Farmer's Restaurant, 115 South La Brea at Manchester, Inglewood, 1958.

Motel, 5547 West Century, Inglewood.

Norm's, Century at Hawthorne, Inglewood, Armét and Davis.

Theme Building, Los Angeles International Airport, 1960.

Milliron's Department Store (now Broadway), Sepulveda at West Eighty-eighth, Westchester, 1949, Gruen and Krummeck.

Snap's, Western at 106th, Los Angeles, 1958, Armét and Davis (rem.).

Tropicana Bowl, 11163 Prairie north of Imperial, Inglewood, 1959, H. W. Underhill.

Thrifty, Imperial near Crenshaw, Inglewood (chain).

Huddle Imperial (now Torch), Imperial at Prairie, Inglewood, Armét and Davis.

Taco Fiesta, Century east of Hawthorne, Inglewood.

Chip's, 590 N. Hawthorne Boulevard, Hawthorne, 1957, Harry Harrison.

Holly's, 13763 Hawthorne Boulevard, Hawthorne, 1956, Armét and Davis.

Jim's Char Burger, El Segundo near Prairie, Hawthorne.

Baskin Robbins, Crenshaw near Rosecrans, Gardena (chain).

El Camino Cafe, 15421 Crenshaw, Gardena (rem.).

Plum's, Crenshaw Boulevard near Artesia Boulevard, Gardena.

LONG BEACH, PALOS VERDES

Shopping center, Pacific Coast Highway at Warner, Huntington Beach, Lloyd Wright.

Palos Verdes Inn, Pacific Coast Highway, Redondo Beach.

Apartments, Pacific Coast Highway near DeGracia, Redondo Beach.

Bowler House, 3456 Via Campesina, Palos Verdes Estates, 1963, Lloyd Wright.

Moore House, 504 Paseo del Mar, Palos Verdes, 1956, Lloyd Wright.

Marineland, West Palos Verdes Drive, Palos Verdes, 1954, Pereira and Luckman (rem.).

Norm's, Pacific Coast Highway at Long Beach, Long Beach, Armét and Davis.

Dimy's, Pacific Coast Highway at Gaviota, Long Beach, 1956, Armét and Davis.

Terry's, San Antonio at Atlantic, Long Beach.

LOS ANGELES: SOUTH CENTRAL

Gas station, Atlantic at Fifty-seventh, Maywood (chain).

Jim's Super Burger, 4356 Slauson, Maywood.

Norm's, Slauson at Malabar, Huntington Park, Armét and Davis.

Peak's (now Hart No. 1), 2850 Slauson Avenue, Huntington Park, 1960 (chain).

Celestial Motel, 5410 South Vermont, Los Angeles.

Norm's, 8511 South Figueroa at Manchester, Los Angeles, 1955, Armét and Davis (rem.).

Stan's Kite Restaurant, 9131 South Vermont at Ninety-second, Los Angeles.

Motel, San Pedro at 102nd, Los Angeles.

Bowl, Central near Imperial, Watts.

Firestone Store, Firestone near Alameda, Southgate (chain).

Arena Bowl, 9203 Atlantic at Southern, Southgate.

Lucky Boy Hamburger Stand, 4135 Firestone Boulevard, Southgate.

Bonanza Family Restaurant, Atlantic at Los Flores, Lynwood (rem.).

Apartment, 3344 Lynwood near Long Beach, Lynwood.

Medical Center, 3625 East Century Boulevard, Lynwood.

Arden Theater, Long Beach Boulevard, Compton, S. Charles Lee.

McDonald's, 981 Rosecrans, Compton, 1957, Stanley C. Meston (rem.) (chain).

Compton Drive-In Theater, 2111 Rosecrans Avenue, Compton.

Compton Carwash, Rosecrans at Bradfield, Compton.

Bethlehem Baptist Church, 4900 South Compton Avenue, Watts, 1944, R. M. Schindler.

DOWNEY, NORWALK, PICO RIVERA

McDonald's 10207 Lakewood at Florence, Downey, 1953, Stanley C. Meston (chain).

Biff's, Rosemead at Telegraph, Pico Rivera (rem.).

McDonald's, Rosemead at Mines, Pico Rivera, 1964, Stanley C. Meston (chain).

Jim's Char Broiled Burgers, Rosemead at Slauson, Pico Rivera.

Sky Villa Motel, 7204 Rosemead Boulevard, Pico Rivera.

Lucky's Hamburgers, Orr and Day near Telegraph, Norwalk.

Norwalk Square Shopping Center sign, Pioneer at Rosecrans, Norwalk, 1950, Stiles O. Clements.

Simpson Buick, Firestone at Dolan, Downey.

Johnie's Broiler, Firestone Boulevard, Downey.

Foxy's Restaurant, Paramount at Third, Downey (chain).

SAN GABRIEL VALLEY

Bob's Big Boy, 1616 East Colorado Boulevard, Pasadena, 1953, S. David Underwood.

Car dealership, 2025 Colorado at San Marino, Pasadena.

Astro Motel, 2800 East Colorado Boulevard, Pasadena (chain).

Gwinn's, 2915 Colorado Boulevard, Pasadena, 1948, Harold Bissner and Harold Zook.

Bullock's Pasadena, 401 South Lake Avenue, Pasadena, 1947, Wurdeman and Becket.

Hamburger stand, Huntington east of Santa Anita, Arcadia.

McDonald's, 563 Foothill Boulevard, Azusa, 1954, Stanley C. Meston (rem.) (chain).

Taco Paco, Foothill Boulevard, Glendora (chain).

Henry's, Garey at Foothill, Pomona, 1957, John Lautner (rem.).

Bowl, Foothill at Vineyard, Cucamonga.

Edward's San Gabriel Drive-In Theater, Valley at Del Mar, San Gabriel.

Car wash, Atlantic at Pomona, Monterey Park (chain).

Taco Village, Alloway at Peck near Ramona, El Monte (prototype).

Medical building, Hacienda at Hayland, La Puente.

Bob's Big Boy, Vincent at Garvey, West Covina, 1958, Armét and Davis (chain).

Covina Bowl, 1060 Rimsdale near Azusa, Covina 1955, Pat DeRosa.

Taco Paco, Glendora near State, West Covina (chain).

McDonald's, 1057 East Mission Boulevard, Pomona, 1954, Stanley C. Meston (chain).

Coral Reef Lounge and Bowl, Holt Avenue, Montclair, 1957, Pat DeRosa.

SAN FERNANDO VALLEY: NORTH

Eichler Homes, Balboa at Jimeno, Granada Hills, 1963, Jones and Emmons.

Mission Hills Bowl, 10430 Sepulveda Boulevard, Mission Hills, 1957, Martin Stern, Jr.

Thrifty, 14727 Rinaldi Street, San Fernando (chain).

Valley House Motel, 9401 Sepulveda Boulevard, Mission Hills.

First Lutheran Church of Northridge, 18355 Roscoe Boulevard, Northridge.

SAN FERNANDO VALLEY: WEST

Bowl, Canoga near Roscoe, Canoga Park.

Thrifty, Roscoe at Topanga Canyon, Canoga Park (chain).

Coffee Dan's (now Bud Raymond's Coffee Shop), Sherman at Etiwanda, Reseda, 1956, Douglas Honnold (rem.).

Bob's Big Boy, 16835 Sherman Way, Reseda, 1956, Richard Rennacker.

Furniture store, Ventura at Oakdale, Tarzana.

Ven-Cino Carwash, Ventura Boulevard, Encino (chain).

SAN FERNANDO VALLEY: CENTRAL

Biff's, 8510 Van Nuys Boulevard, Panorama City, 1950, Honnold and Rex (rem.).

Bob's Big Boy, 8300 Van Nuys Boulevard, Panorama City, Honnold and Rex (rem.).

Panorama Bowl, Van Nuys north of Roscoe, Panorama City.

Great Western Savings, Van Nuys at Titus, Van Nuys.

Bob's Big Boy, 5355 Van Nuys Boulevard, Van Nuys, 1959, Wayne McAllister.

Stanley Burke's (now Lamplighter), 5043 Van Nuys Boulevard, Van Nuys, 1958, Armét and Davis (rem.).

Denny's, Sherman at Van Nuys, Van Nuys, 1958, Armét and Davis (rem.) (chain).

Coffee Dan's, Van Nuys Boulevard, Van Nuys, 1958, Palmer and Krisel (rem.).

Kerry's, 14846 Ventura Boulevard, Sherman Oaks, 1953.

Chinese American Food, Victory at Babcock, Van Nuys.

Casa de Cadillac, 14401 Ventura Boulevard, Sherman Oaks, 1950, Conklin and Coleman.

Sultan Carwash, Woodman Boulevard, Van Nuys.

SAN FERNANDO VALLEY: EAST

Car wash, Laurel Canyon at Ventura, Studio City, 1960, Armét and Davis.

Tiny Naylor's, 12056 Ventura at Laurel Canyon, Studio City, 1961, Ron Cleveland.

DuPar's, Ventura at Laurel Canyon, Studio City.

Peak's (now Chuck Burger), 6506 Laurel Canyon near Victory, Studio City, 1961 (chain).

High-rise, Victory at Bellingham, Studio City, 1960, Honnold and Rex.

Allstate Savings, 5077 Lankershim Boulevard, North Hollywood.

Car wash and coffee shop, 5964 Laurel Canyon at Oxnard, North Hollywood, 1960 (chain).

Denny's, Lankershim at Burbank, North Hollywood, 1960, Armét and Davis (chain).

BURBANK

Ralph's Market, Victory at Buena Vista, Burbank.

Union Hall, 2300 Victory near Buena Vista, Burbank, 1958, Smith and Williams.

Car wash, Magnolia near Victory, Burbank (chain).

Sand's Cleaners, Magnolia at Rose, Burbank (chain).

Bob's Big Boy, Riverside at Alameda, Toluca Lake, 1949, Wayne McAllister.

Orange Julius, Olive at alameda, Burbank (rem.) (chain).

GLENDALE

Glendale Federal Savings, 401 North Brand.

Car dealership, Colorado east of Glendale, 1947, John Lautner (rem.).

Bob's Big Boy, 1000 Colorado Street, 1951, Wayne McAllister (rem.).

Flower shop, Los Feliz east of Glendale.

ORANGE COUNTY: ANAHEIM, GARDEN GROVE

Anaheim Bowl, 1925 West Lincoln, Anaheim, 1957, Pat DeRosa.

Sapce Age Lodge, 1176 West Katella Avenue near West, Anaheim (chain).

Eden Roc Motel, West Street, Anaheim.

Bob's Big Boy, Garden Grove at Gilbert, Garden Grove, 1958, Armét and Davis (chain).

Garden Grove Community Church compound, 12141 Lewis Street, Garden Grove.

Drive-in Church, 1959, Richard Neutra;

Drive-in Cathedral, 1978, Philip Johnson.

Wichstand menu. The Wichstand operations, like those of Carolina Pines, had been drive-ins in the thirties which that updated to coffee shops in the fifties.

THE WICH STAND

FIGUEROA AT FLORENCE • SLAUSON AT OVERHILL • LOS ANGELES

COFFEE SHOP • DRIVE IN • DINING ROOM • COCKTAILS • COFFEE SHOP • DRIVE IN • DINING ROOM • COCKTAILS

bibliography

A. D. Profiles: Bruce Goff. London: Architectural Design, 1978.

Atkin, William Wilson, and Adler, Joan. *Interiors Book of Restaurants.* New York: Whitney Library of Design, 1960.

Banham, Reyner. *Los Angeles: The Architecture of Four Ecologies.* Baltimore: Penguin Books, 1973.

Bayley, Stephen. *Harley Earl and the Dream Machine.* New York: Alfred A. Knopf, 1983.

Blake, Peter. *God's Own Junkyard.* New York: Holt Rinehart and Winston, 1964.

Corn, Joseph J., and Horrigan, Brian. *Yesterday's Tomorrows.* New York: Summit Books, 1984.

Gebhard, David, and Von Breton, Harriette. *L.A. in the Thirties.* Salt Lake City: Peregrine Smith, Inc., 1975.

———*Lloyd Wright Architect.* Exhibit catalog, The Regents, University of California, 1971.

Gebhard, David, and Winter, Robert. *Architecture in Los Angeles: A Compleat Guide.* Salt Lake City: Gibbs M. Smith, Inc., 1985.

Greenberg, Cara. *Mid-Century Modern: Furniture of the 1950s.* New York: Harmony Books, 1984.

Gutman, Richard J. S., and Kaufman, Elliott. *American Diner.* New York: Harper & Row, 1979.

Haskell, Douglas. "Architecture and Popular Taste." *Architectural Forum,* August 1958.

———"Googie Architecture." *House and Home,* February 1952.

Heimann, Jim; Georges, Rip; and Gebhard, David. *California Crazy.* San Francisco: Chronicle Books, 1980.

Hess, Alan. "Eichler Homes." *Arts and Architecture.* Vol. 3, No. 3, 1984.

———"John Lautner's Mauer House." *Fine Homebuilding,* December/January 1983–84.

Hirshorn, Paul, and Izenour, Steven. *White Towers.* Cambridge, Mass: MIT Press, 1979.

Hitchcock, Henry-Russell. "An Eastern Critic Looks at Western Architecture." *California Arts and Architecture.* December 1940.

———*In the Nature of Materials: The Buildings of Frank Lloyd Wright 1887–1941.* New York: Hawthorn Books, 1942.

Jackson, J. B. *Discovering the Vernacular Landscape.* New Haven, Conn: Yale University Press, 1984.

———*Landscapes.* Boston: The University of Massachusetts Press, 1970.

Kroc, Ray. *Grinding It Out: The Making of McDonald's.* New York: Berkley Publishing Corporation, 1977.

McWilliams, Carey. *Southern California: An Island on the Land.* Salt Lake City: Peregrine Smith, Inc., 1973.

Moore, Charles, and Allen, Gerald. *Dimensions: Space, Shape and Scale in Architecture.* New York: Architectural Record Books, 1976.

Oliver, Richard, and Ferguson, Nancy. "Place, Product, Packaging." *Architectural Record.* February 1978.

Philadelphia Museum of Art. *Design Since 1945.* Exhibit catalog, 1983.

Silk, Gerald. *Automobile and Culture.* New York: Harry N. Abrams, Inc., 1984.

Venturi, Robert; Scott Brown, Denise; and Izenour, Steven. *Learning from Las Vegas.* Cambridge, Mass: The MIT Press, 1972.

Vieyra, Daniel I. *Fill 'er Up: An Architectural History of America's Gas Stations.* New York: Collier Books, 1979.

Wolfe, Tom. "Electrographic Architecture." *Architectural Design.* July 1969.

———*The Kandy-Kolored Tangerine-Flake Streamline Baby.* New York: Farrar, Straus & Giroux, 1965.

index